《中国节庆文化》丛书
编委会名单

顾　问

史蒂文·施迈德　　冯骥才　　周明甫

黄忠彩　　武翠英　　王国泰

主　编

李　松

副主编

张　刚　　彭新良

编　委（按姓氏笔画排列）

王学文　　田　阡　　邢　莉　　齐勇锋

李　旭　　李　松　　杨正文　　杨海周

张　刚　　张　勃　　张　跃　　张　暖

金　蕾　　赵学玉　　萧　放　　彭新良

List of Members of Editorial Board
of *Chinese Festival Culture Series*

中国节庆文化丛书

Chinese Festival Culture Series

The Festival of March the Third

主 编 李 松
副主编 张 刚 彭新良

三月三

田 阡
石 甜 ◎ 著
罗红云
罗天霞 ◎ 译

全 国 百 佳 图 书 出 版 单 位

时代出版传媒股份有限公司
安徽人民出版社

图书在版编目(CIP)数据

三月三:汉英对照/田阡,石甜著;罗红云,罗天霞译.—合肥:安徽人民出版社,2014.1(中国节庆文化丛书/李松,张刚,彭新良主编)

ISBN 978－7－212－07063－2

Ⅰ.①三… Ⅱ.①田… ②石… ③罗… ④罗 Ⅲ.①节日—风俗习惯—中国—汉、英 Ⅳ.①K892.1

中国版本图书馆 CIP 数据核字(2013)第 315294 号

Zhongguo Jieqing Wenhua Congshu　　Sanyuesan
中国节庆文化丛书　三月三

李　松　主编　张　刚　彭新良　副主编
田　阡　石　甜　著　罗红云　罗天霞　译

出　版　人:朱寒冬　　　　　　图书策划:胡正义　丁怀超　李　旭
责任编辑:刘　超　　　　　　　装帧设计:宋文岚

出版发行:时代出版传媒股份有限公司 http://www.press-mart.com
　　　　　安徽人民出版社 http://www.ahpeople.com
　　　　　合肥市政务文化新区翡翠路 1118 号出版传媒广场八楼
　　　　　邮编:230071
　　　　　营销部电话:0551-63533258　0551-63533292(传真)
制　　　版:合肥市中旭制版有限责任公司
印　　　制:安徽新华印刷股份有限公司

开本:710×1010　1/16　　　印张:12.5　　　字数:220 千
版次:2014 年 3 月第 1 版　　2016 年 7 月第 4 次印刷

标准书号:ISBN 978－7－212－07063－2　　定价:24.00 元

Our Common Days

(Preface)

The most important day for a person in a year is his or her birthday, and the most important days for all of us are the festivals. We can say that the festivals are our common days.

Festivals are commemorating days with various meanings. There are national, ethnic and religious festivals, such as the National Day and Christmas Day, and some festivals for certain groups, such as the Women's Day, the Children's Day and the Labor Day. There are some other festivals closely related to our lives. These festivals have long histories and different customs that have been passed on from one generation to another. There are also different traditional festivals. China is a country full of 56 ethnic groups, and all of the ethnic groups are collectively called the Chinese Nation. Some traditional festivals are common to all people of the Chinese Nation, and some others are unique to certain ethnic groups. For example, the Spring Festival, the Mid-Autumn Day, the Lantern Festival, the Dragon Boat Festival, the Tomb-Sweeping Day and the Double-Ninth Day are common festivals to all of the Chinese people. On the other hand, the New Year of the Qiang Ethnic (a World Cultural Heritage), for example, is a unique festival to the

我们共同的日子

（代序）

个人一年一度最重要的日子是生日，大家一年一度最重要的日子是节日。节日是大家共同的日子。

节日是一种纪念日，内涵多种多样。有民族的、国家的、宗教的，比如国庆节、圣诞节等。有某一类人的，如妇女、儿童、劳动者的，这便是妇女节、儿童节、劳动节等。也有与人们的生活生产密切相关的，这类节日历史悠久，很早就形成了一整套人们约定俗成、代代相传的节日习俗，这是一种传统的节日。传统节日也多种多样。中国是个多民族国家，有五十六个民族，统称中华民族。传统节日有全民族共有的，也有某个民族特有的。比如春节、中秋节、元宵节、端午节、清明节、重阳节等，就为中华民族所共用和共享；世界文化遗产羌年就为羌族独有和独享。各民族这样的节日很多。

　　传统节日是在漫长的农耕时代形成的。农耕时代生产与生活、人与自然的关系十分密切。人们或为了感恩于大自然的恩赐，或为了庆祝辛苦劳作换来的收获，或为了激发生命的活力，或为了加强人际的亲情，经过长期相互认同，最终约定俗成，渐渐把一年中某一天确定为节日，并创造了十分完整又严格的节俗，如仪式、庆典、规制、禁忌，乃至特定的游艺、装饰与食品，来把节日这天演化成一个独具内涵的迷人的日子。更重要的是，人们在每一个传统的节日里，还把共同的生活理想、人间愿望与审美追求融入节日的内涵与种种仪式中。因此，它是中华民族世间理想与生活愿望极致的表现。可以说，我们的传统——精神文化传统，往往就是依靠这代代相传的一年一度的节日继承下来的。

Qiang Ethnic Group, and there are many festivals celebrated only by minorities in China.

The traditional festivals are formed throughout the long agrarian age, during which the relationships between life and production and between the people and the nature were very close. To express the gratitude to the nature for its gifts, or celebrate the harvests from hard works, or stimulate the vitality of life, or strengthen the relationships among people, people would determine one day in a year as a festival with complete and strict customs, such as ceremonies, rules and taboos, special activities, decorations and foods to make the festival a day with unique meanings and charms. More importantly, people would integrate their good wishes into the meanings and ceremonies of the festivals. Therefore, the festivals could represent the ideals and wishes of the people in the best way. It is safe to say that our traditions, more specifically, our spiritual and cultural traditions, are inherited through the festivals year by year.

However, since the 20th century, with the transition from the agricultural civilization to the industrial civilization, the cultural traditions formed during the agrarian age have begun to collapse. Especially in China, during the process of opening up in the past 100 years, the festival culture, especially the festival culture in cities, has been impacted by the modern civilization and foreign cultures. At present, the Chinese people have felt that the traditional festivals are leaving away day by day so that some worries are produced about this. With the diminishing of the traditional festivals, the traditional spirits carried by them will also disappear. However, we are not just watching them disappearing, but actively dealing with them, which could fully represent the self-consciousness of the Chinese people in terms of culture.

In those ten years, with the fully launching of the folk culture heritage rescue program of China, and the promotion of the application for national non-material cultural heritage list, more attention has been paid to the traditional festivals, some of which have been added to the central cultural heritage list. After that, in 2006, China has determined that the second Saturday of June of each year shall be the Cultural Heritage Day, and in 2007, the State Council added three important festivals, namely the Tomb-sweeping Day, the Dragon Boat Festival and the Mid-Autumn Day, as the legal holidays. These decisions have showed that our government

然而，自从二十世纪整个人类进入了由农耕文明向工业文明的过渡，农耕时代形成的文化传统开始瓦解。尤其是中国，在近百年由封闭走向开放的过程中，节日文化——特别是城市的节日文化受到现代文明与外来文化的冲击。当下人们已经鲜明地感受到传统节日渐行渐远，并为此产生忧虑。传统节日的淡化必然使其中蕴含的传统精神随之涣散。然而，人们并没有坐等传统的消失，主动和积极地与之应对。这充分显示了当代中国人在文化上的自觉。

近十年，随着中国民间文化遗产抢救工程的全面展开，国家非物质文化遗产名录申报工作的有力推动，传统节日受到关注，一些重要的传统节日列入了国家文化遗产名录。继而，2006年国家将每年六月的第二个周六确定为"文化遗产日"；2007年国务院决定将三个中华民族的重要节日——清明节、端午节和中秋节列为法定放假日。这一重大决定，表现了国家对公众的传统文化生活及其传承的重视与尊重，同时也是保护节日文化遗产十分必要的措施。

节日不放假必然直接消解了节日文化，放假则是恢复节日传统的首要条件。但放假不等于远去的节日立即就会回到身边。节日与假日的不同是因为节日有特定的文化内容与文化形式。那么，重温与恢复已经变得陌生的传统节日习俗则是必不可少的了。

千百年来，我们的祖先从生活的愿望出发，为每一个节日都创造出许许多多美丽又动人的习俗。这种愿望是理想主义的，所以节日习俗是理想的；愿望是情感化的，所以节日习俗也是情感化的；愿望是美好的，所以节日习俗是美的。人们用合家团聚的年夜饭迎接新年；把天上的明月化为手中甜甜的月饼，来象征人间的团圆；在严寒刚刚消退、万物复苏的早春，赶到野外去打扫墓地，告慰亡灵，

emphasizes and respects the traditional cultural activities and their heritages. Meanwhile, these are important measures to protect festival cultural heritages.

Festivals without holidays will directly harm the festival culture. Holiday is the most important condition for the recovery of a festival, but holiday does not mean that the festival will come back immediately. Festivals are different from holidays because festivals have unique cultural contents and forms. Therefore, it will be necessary to review and recover the customs of the traditional festivals that have become strange to us.

For thousands of years, our ancestors created beautiful and moving customs for each festival based on their best wishes. The customs are ideal, since the wishes are ideal. The customs are emotional, since the wishes are emotional. The customs are beautiful, since the wishes are beautiful. We have the family reunion dinner to receive a new year. We make moon cakes according to the shape of the moon in the mid-autumn to symbolize the reunion of our family. We visit the tombs of our ancestors in the early spring and go outing to beautiful and green hills to express our grief. These beautiful festival customs have offered us great comfort and peace for generations.

Our Common Days

To ethnic minorities, their unique festivals are of more importance, since these festivals bear their common memories and represent their spirits, characters and identities.

Who ever can say that the traditional customs are out of date? If we have forgotten these customs, we should review them. The review is not imitating the customs of our ancients, but experiencing the spirits and emotions of the traditions with our heart.

During the course of history, customs are changing, but the essence of the national tradition will not change. The tradition is to constantly pursue a better life, to be thankful to the nature and to express our best wishes for family reunion and the peace of the world.

This is the theme of our festivals, and the reason and purpose of this series of books.

The planning and compiling of the series is unique. All of the festivals are held once a year. Since China is a traditional agricultural society,

表达心中的缅怀，同时戴花插柳，踏青春游，亲切地拥抱大地山川……这些诗意化的节日习俗，使我们一代代人的心灵获得了美好的安慰与宁静。

对于少数民族来说，他们特有的节日的意义则更加重要。节日还是他们民族集体记忆的载体、共同精神的依托、个性的表现、民族身份之所在。

谁说传统的习俗过时了？如果我们淡忘了这些习俗，就一定要去重温一下传统。重温不是表象地模仿古人的形式，而是用心去体验传统中的精神与情感。

在历史的进程中，习俗是在不断变化的，但民族传统的精神本质不应变。这传统就是对美好生活不懈的追求，对大自然的感恩与敬畏，对家庭团圆与世间和谐永恒的企望。

这便是我们节日的主题，也是这套节庆丛书编写的根由与目的。

这套书的筹划独具匠心。所有节日都是一年一次。由于我国为传统农耕社会，所以生活与生产同步，节日与大自然的节气密切相关。本丛书以一年的春、夏、秋、冬四个时间板块，将纷繁的传统节日清晰有序地排列开来，又总揽成书，既包括全民族共有的节日盛典，也把少数民族重要的节日遗产纳入其中，以周详的文献和生动的传说，将每个节日的源起、流布与习俗，亦图亦文、有滋有味地娓娓道来。一节一册，单用方便，放在一起则是中华民族传统节日的一部全书，既有知识性、资料性、工具性，又有阅读性和趣味性。这样一套丛书不仅是对我国传统节日的一次总结，也是对传统节日文化富于创意的弘扬。

我读了书稿，心生欣喜，因序之。

冯骥才
2013.12.25

the life is synchronized with production, and the festivals are closely relevant to the climates. In this series, all of the traditional festivals in China will be introduced in the order of the four seasons, covering the common festivals as well as important ethnic festivals that have been listed as cultural heritages. All of the festivals are described in detail with texts and images to introduce their origins, customs and distribution. Each book of the series is used to introduce one festival so that it is convenient to read individually and it may be regarded as a complete encyclopedia if connected with each other. Therefore, it is not only intellectual, informative and instrumental, but also readable and interesting. The series could be used as a tool book or read for leisure. It is not only the summary of the traditional festivals of our country, but an innovative promotion of our traditional festival culture.

I felt very delighted after reading the manuscript, so I wrote this preface.

Feng Jicai
December 25th, 2013

目　录 / Contents

第一章　传承
Chapter One　Inheritance

❶ 早期起源
The Early Origin
/003

❷ 魏晋时期
The Wei and Jin Dynasties
/013

❸ 隋唐时期
The Sui and Tang Dynasties
/021

❹ 宋元时期
The Song and Yuan Dynasties
/029

❺ 少数民族
Ethnic Minorities
/036

第二章　流布
Chapter Two　Circulation

❶ 河洛中原
Heluo Central Plain
/047

❷ 边陲之地
Frontier Land
/053

❸ 多彩民族
Colorful Minorities
/077

目 录

第三章　风俗
Chapter Three　Customs

❶ 流觞、流卵、流枣
Floating Goblets,Eggs and Dates /109

❷ 插柳踏青
Wearing Willow and Spring Outing /113

❸ 饮食习俗
Diet Customs /115

❹ 载歌载舞
Singing and Dancing /127

第四章　特色节庆地
Chapter Four　Places of Characteristic Celebration

❶ 江都"三月三"庙会
March 3rd Temple Fair in Jiangdu /149

❷ 黎族非物质文化遗产：三月三
Li People's intangible Culture Heritage: March 3rd /155

❸ 乌江镇的三月三
March 3rd of Wujiang Town /158

❹ 侗家的"播种节"
Dong People's Seed Sowing Festival /162

❺ 荔枝湾，三月三
March 3rd of Lizhiwan /169

❻ 曲江上巳节
Winding River Shangsi Festival /178

❼ 朝拜
Pilgrimage /180

《中国节庆文化》丛书后记
The Postscript of *Chinese Festival Culture Series* /187

第一章 传承

年年有个三月三，王母娘娘庆寿诞；各路神仙来上寿，蟠桃美酒会神仙

——北京童谣

中国自古有"二月二，龙抬头；三月三，生轩辕"的说法，实际上，三月三的起源不仅来自中华民族始祖之一的黄帝，还与伏羲、西王母等神话传说人物有关。在历史长河中，三月三逐渐被固定下来作为"上巳"节来庆祝，又慢慢地与寒食节、清明节融合在一起。

Chapter one

Inheritance

It's March 3rd every year, and the Goddess of Heaven celebrates her birthday; all gods come to congratulate her and they get together in the feast of peaches and delicious wine.

——Beijing Children's Ballad

There has been the saying that "the dragon raises its head on February 2rd and Xuanyuan was born on March 3rd"; in fact, the origin of March 3rd comes from the Yellow Emperor, who was one of Chinese ancestors, and was related to the legendary characters such as Fuxi and Queen of the West. In the long history, March 3rd has been fixed and celebrated as Shangsi Festival gradually and has been integrated with Cold Food Festival and Tomb-Sweeping Festival.

1 早期起源
The Early Origin

Each nation often describes beautiful and fair-sounding legends of clans in the ancient times and how they have lived and multiplied on this land, and the Yellow Emperor is this type of legendary character. It's debatable whether the Yellow Emperor existed and whether he was a hero or the title of a clan. *National Language: Jin Language* recorded that, "Shaodian married a woman called Youjiao, who gave birth to the Yellow Emperor and the Yan Emperor. The Yellow Emperor grew up in Ji Water, and the Yan Emperor grew up in Jiang River (Qingjiang River in Baoji, Shaanxi). They were talented people when they became adults. Therefore, the Yellow Emperor was called Ji, and the Yan Emperor was called Jiang. The two emperors helped each other with armies, because they were talented people."

每个民族往往都用优美动听的远古传说来讲述族群的传说，怎样在这片土地上生活繁衍至今，黄帝就是这类传说人物。黄帝是否真的存在过，他是一个英雄还是一个氏族部落的称号，这些都是有争议的。《国语·晋语》载："昔少典娶于有蟜氏，生黄帝、炎帝。黄帝以姬水成，炎帝以姜水（今陕西宝鸡清姜河）成。成而异德，故黄帝为姬，炎帝为姜。二帝用师以相济也，异德之故也。"

根据上古神话传说，黄帝由其母附宝感大电而生：

（黄帝）母曰附宝，见大电绕北斗枢星，照郊野，感附宝，孕二十四月。生黄帝于寿丘，长于姬水，有圣德，受国于有熊，居轩辕之丘，故因以为名，又以为号[1]。

According to the myth and legend in the ancient times, the Yellow Emperor was born by his mother after being inspired by the large lightning:

The name of the mother (of the Yellow Emperor) was Fubao. She saw the large lightning which was around the Plough and shone the wild fields, and she was enlightened and was pregnant for twenty four months. The Yellow Emperor was born in Shouqiu, grew up in Ji Water, had holy virtues, set up his state in Youxiong, lived in the hill of Xuanyuan, so he used Xuanyuan as his name and style name[1].

[1]柏明、李颖科《黄帝与黄帝陵》，西北大学出版社，1990年03月第1版，第9页

[1]The Yellow Emperor and the Yellow Emperor Mausoleum, Bai Ming / March 1990, Version 1, p9

The Yellow Emperor Xuanyuan was the son of Shaodian, so his original name was Gongsun, and his style name was Xuanyuan because he changed his family name as Ji and lived on the hill of Xuanyuan, which is located in the northwest of Xinzhen of Hunan at present and the location of which is disputable. He displayed his outstanding talent soon after his birth, and *Records of the Historian* wrote that, "He was bright when he was born, was good at talking when he was a baby, had a modest style of doing things and an upright character when he was young; in his youth, he was honest and possessed a strong ability of distinguishing what was right and what was wrong. He was brilliant when he grew up." He could talk soon after he was born, and he could do everything when he was fifteen years old. It was said that he invented many production tools, sowed cereals, grass and trees, invented vessel, vehicle and cart of compass, established algorithm and melody etc., and ordered his civil officials to invent Chinese hieroglyphs. The Yellow Emperor made these brilliant achievements, he and the Yan Emperor of another clan in Jiang River were called the ancestors of China. In order to commemorate the humane primogenitors, therefore the later generations chose the birthday of the Yellow Emperor to hold sacrifice and celebration for them.

There is another saying that people commemorate Fuxi on March 3rd. Fuxi was also called Mixi, Paoxi, Xihuang, Huangxi, Taihao, Baoxi, but he

轩辕黄帝是少典之子，本姓公孙，长居姬水，因改姓姬，居轩辕之丘（在今河南新郑西北，有争议），故号轩辕氏。黄帝出生后不久就展示出过人的才能，《史记》里说他"生而神灵，弱而能言，幼而徇齐，长而敦敏，成而聪明"，他生下没多久就会开口说话，15岁的时候已经无所不能了，据说发明了诸多生产工具，播百谷草木，创造了舟车指南车，制定了算数、音律等，还令手下文官发明了文字。这些都是黄帝的辉煌成就，黄帝与另外一个部落氏族——姜水的炎帝被称为华夏始祖。后人为了纪念华夏族的人文始祖，选择在黄帝诞辰这一天举办祭祀庆祝活动，来铭记他们。

关于三月三，还有一种说法是为了纪念伏羲氏。伏羲又被称作宓羲、庖牺（亦称庖牺氏），亦称牺皇、皇羲、太昊、包犠，史记中称伏羲，他被认为是人类的祖先，是三

皇之首，开天辟地的第一人。传说中，伏羲是人首蛇身，和妹妹女娲捏土造人，繁衍后代，是人类的始祖。据说，伏羲生于陇西成纪（今甘肃天水），徙治陈仓，都于陈宛丘（今河南淮阳），他教民结网，渔猎畜牧，制造八卦等，豫东一带尊称伏羲为"人祖爷"，在淮阳（伏羲建都地）建起太昊陵古庙，由农历二月二到三月三为太昊陵庙会，善男信女，南船北马，都云集陵区，朝拜人祖。

was called Fuxi in *Records of the Historian* and was thought as the ancestor of human beings, the head of the three emperors, and the first person since the genesis of the heaven and the earth. In the legend, Fuxi had a human head and a snake body. He and his sister Nüwa made human beings with clay, repopulated the earth and they were the ancestors of human beings. It was said that Fuxi was born in Chengji of Longxi (Tianshui of Gansu today). He resettled and ruled in Chengcang, and founded a capital in Chenwanqiu (Huiyang of Hunan today). He taught people netting, fishing, hunting and ranching, and made the Eight Diagrams. Fuxi was called "Human Ancestor" in the area of Eastern Henan Province, where ancient Taihao Mausoleum Temple was established in Huaiyang (the place of the capital of Fuxi). Taihao Mausoleum Temple Fair was held from lunar February 2nd to March 3rd, when Buddhist devotees got together in the mausoleum by ship from the south or by horse from the north and worshiped the human ancestor.

It was said that the Goddess of Heaven held the heavenly peach banquet on lunar March 3rd. In the legend of the ancient times, she was a female character, and *Mountain and Sea Classics* described that she had the image of semi-human and semi-animal, "The Goddess of Heaven had the shape of human, with a leopard tail and tiger teeth. She was good at shouting. She had untidy hair, wore a square hat on her head, and mastered disasters and penalties on the heaven," and she was the goddess mastering disasters and penalties. Since the Han Dynasty, especially the Wei and Jin Dynasties, the image of the Goddess of Heaven became graceful and dignified, as the *Inner Story of Emperor Wu of the Han Dynasty* described that she was a goddess with beautiful appearance, who lived in the western wonderland, and bestowed Emperor Wu of the Han Dynasty a peach which became ripe after three thousand years. In latter literary works, the Goddess of Heaven held her birthday party when peaches became ripe, and invited gods to congratulate her birthday, and this was the origin of March 3rd.

When the Goddess of Heaven celebrated her birthday on Zhongnan Mountain on March 3rd that year, gods in the heaven came to congratulate her, and she treated them cordially. A god reported suddenly that, "Lü Dongbin comes." The Goddess of Heaven hated Lü Dongbin, so her face turned firm, and she said, "Don't let Lü Dongbin come to see me." After hearing her words, he said angrily, "I

农历三月初三，还是传说中王母娘娘举办蟠桃会的时间。王母娘娘是上古神话传说中一位女性人物，《山海经》把她描述成一位半人半兽形象，"西王母其状如人，豹尾虎齿，善啸，蓬发戴胜，是司天之厉及五残"，她是掌管灾厉和刑杀的神祇。从汉代以后尤其是魏晋时期，西王母的形象变成了一位儒雅高贵的女神，《汉武帝内传》谓她是容貌绝世的女神，住在西方的瑶池仙境，并赐给汉武帝三千年结一次果的蟠桃。在后来的文学作品中，王母娘娘在蟠桃成熟的时候会举行寿筵，宴请诸位神仙来贺寿，这就是三月三的来源。

那年三月三日王母娘娘在终南山过生日，天上的神仙都来祝贺，王母娘娘盛情接待。有神忽报："吕洞宾来了"。王母娘娘讨厌吕洞宾，把脸一沉说："不要吕洞宾来见我。"吕洞宾听后，很生气说："我偏要去！"他问王母娘娘："众仙都来参加盛会，为何不要我来呢？"王母娘娘说："你是个好酒色财气之神，我不喜欢你来。"

吕洞宾哈哈大笑，他追问王母娘娘："请当着众神仙说说我怎么是个酒色财气之神呢？"王母娘娘说："上次蟠桃会，你喝醉了酒，不是贪酒是什么？"吕洞宾说："娘娘说的不对，是娘娘举行的寿宴大会，让众仙饮酒作乐，不叫我喝我怎会醉呢？"王母娘娘又说："你三戏白牡丹，传扬众仙，难道这不是好色吗？"吕洞宾笑道："我是相爱，并无妒心，娘娘是个女神，都比我严重。"王母一听，斥责吕洞宾说："不要胡言乱讲！"吕洞宾说："我有事实，牛郎和织女，情投意合，要结为夫妻，娘娘你却嫉妒吃醋。扔出玉簪划了一道天河，将一对夫妻分开，一年只许他们见一次，这是多么缺德呀？"王母娘娘脸都气黑了。

insist on coming!" He asked the Goddess of Heaven, "Why don't you let me come when all gods come to the party?" The Goddess of Heaven said, "I don't want you to come because you are a god who likes wine, women and money."

Lü Dongbin laughed and he continued to ask the Goddess of Heaven, "Please explain to all the gods why I am a god liking wine and money?" The Goddess of Heaven said, "Doesn't the fact that you became drunk mean that you like drinking?" Lü Dongbin said that, "You are wrong. You held the birthday banquet and let all gods drink and have fun. How can I become drunk if you don't let me drink?" The Goddess of Heaven said, "You flirted with the White Peony thrice and told all gods, which indeed explains that you are amorous." Lü Dongbin answered, "I believe in love and don't envy others. You are a goddess, but you are worse than me." Hearing this, the Goddess of Heaven scolded him, "Nonsense!" Lü Dongbin said, "I have the fact that Cowherd and Weaving Girl loved each other and wanted to marry, but you envied them. You took out your jade hairpin and divided a sky river, separated them from each other, and allowed them to meet each other once a year. You are so wicked!" The face of the Goddess of Heaven turned black.

The Goddess of Heaven paused and asked Lü Dongbin, "I heard that you grabbed a lot of treasures when the Eight Immortals crossed the sea and made trouble in the Dragon Palace, didn't you?" Lü Dongbin answered, "The Jade Emperor gave the order that each god shows his or her special prowess as the Eight Immortals crossing the sea. You cannot scold me because he made clear beforehand." The Goddess of Heaven said, "I lived in the fairy palace. How can I be greedy?" Lü Dongbin said, "You hold your birthday party on March 3rd every year luxuriously, and all gods visit you with presents, and you accept them. Aren't you extortionary and greedy?" The Goddess of Heaven quivered with rage. She pointed at the nose of Lü Dongbin and said, "Gods shall not do things in anger, but you often make this mistake. You waved your treasured sword and killed deliberately when the Eight Immortals crossed the sea. How can you kill others without anger?" Lü Dongbin waved his head and laughed, "The Goddess of Heaven! I accomplished with one effort, fought enemies, and made battle achievements! It's easy for you to be angry indeed!" The Goddess of Heaven continued to ask, "How can you prove it?" He said, "I am an inferior god, but you are a superior goddess, and you like to find faults of inferior gods. You refuse me to come, and you're afraid of my true words. How can you do in this way without anger?" The

王母娘娘停了一会儿，又问吕洞宾："八仙过海，大闹龙宫时，据说你抢了龙宫不少财宝，是与不是？"吕洞宾哈哈笑说："玉帝传旨，八仙过海，各显神通嘛，吩咐有言在先，怎能怪我呢？"王母说："我身居仙宫，怎能贪呢？"吕洞宾说："每年三月三，你张扬祝寿，凡来参加的神仙无不携带礼品，你都接受，这不是勒索贪财吗？"王母娘娘气得浑身打哆嗦，指着吕洞宾的鼻子说："神的事情，不能意气行事，你常犯这个毛病，八仙过海时，你挥动宝剑，有意砍杀，你不是动气怎能砍杀呢？"吕洞宾摇头发笑，说道："王母娘，我是一鼓作气，奋战杀敌，那是战功！你才最爱动气哩！"王母娘娘追问："有何为证？"吕洞宾说："我是个下等仙，你是上天的娘娘，你光找下面的毛病，你不肯要我来，是怕我说

实话，你不动气能这样做吗?"说得王母娘娘拂袖而去[①]。

王母娘娘寿诞时，民间举行盛大的庙会庆祝，"三月初三春正长，蟠桃宫里看烧香；沿河一带风微起，十丈红尘匝地扬"（《都门杂咏》）。

Goddess of Heaven brushed her sleeves and left[①].

When the Goddess of Heaven celebrates her birthday, people hold grand temple fair to celebrate it on the earth, "It's the fair spring on March 3rd; the gods in the Heavenly Peach Palace watch people burning incenses; the breeze blows in the riverside, and a lot of red dust fly from the ground" (*Miscellaneous Praise of Dumen*).

①雪犁 等主编，《中华民俗源流集成（节日岁时卷）》，甘肃人民出版社，1994年，第130-131页

①Collection of Chinese Folk Customs and Sources (Volume of Holidays and Seasons), pp130-131.

There is another reason for people to celebrate March 3rd, which say that Goddess Nüwa made human beings on this day. Goddess Nüwa , who was the sister of Fuxi, was the genesis goddess in the legend of the ancient times, as she made human beings with clay, created the human society, melted five-colored stones to patch up the sky broken by Gonggong, made the heaven, the earth and all things, and brought life to the world. It was said that Nüwa made animals and human beings according to the time order: the first day was the chick day, the second day was the dog day, the third day was the sheep day, the fourth day was the pig day, the fifth day was the ox day, the sixth day was the horse day, and the seventh day was the human day. According to the calculation of the heavenly stems and earthly branches, March 3rd was Si Day, which was "the human day". People make "seven-treasure porridge" and make pancake called "Xuntian", and people in some places hold large-scale temple fairs and sacrifice activities to commemorate Goddess Nüwa for endowing life on this day.

人们庆祝三月初三，还有一个原因，据说这一天是女娲娘娘创造出人类的日子。女娲娘娘是伏羲的妹妹，在上古神话传说中是创世女神，她用泥土捏成了人类，创造了人类社会，又熔炼五色石，把共工撞坏的苍天给修补好，还造了天地万物，给世间带来生命。相传，女娲造人时，按照时间顺序捏成动物和人类，初一是鸡日、初二是狗日、初三为羊日、初四为猪日、初五为牛日、初六是马日、初七为人日。按照天干地支来算，三月初三刚好是巳日，也就是"人日"。在这一天，人们要熬制"七宝羹"，做一种名为"薰天"的煎饼，有些地方的老百姓还举办大型庙会和祭祀活动来纪念给予生命的女娲娘娘。

在瑶族同胞聚居的地区，三月三是纪念瑶族祖先盘古的日子。相传在很久以前，瑶族的英雄盘古为了制服前来瑶寨伤人的猛兽，不幸被羚羊用角顶破肚子，当场死亡。全寨的人都非常伤心，那一天正好是三月初三，于是为了铭记瑶族人民的英雄，就把每年的三月初三作为纪念盘古的日子，这一天也叫"干巴节"。

March 3rd is the day to commemorate Pangu who was the ancestor of Yao people in the regions where Yao people live. It was said that Pangu, the hero of Yao people, came to Yao Village to fight the furious animals, but his stomach was broken by the horns of an antelope and was dead on the scene long long ago. All villagers were sad and that day was March 3rd, so they used that day to commemorate Pangu who was the hero of Yao people every year, and it was also called Ganba Festival.

2 魏晋时期
The Wei and Jin Dynasties

As early as the pre-Qin Dynasty, people had the habit to clean their bodies and get rid of dust in rivers in spring. *Extensive Records of the Taiping Era* recorded that Yue people offered two women when King Zhao of the Zhou Dynasty had ascended the throne for twenty years. One was called Yanjuan, and the other was called Yanyu. They were slim and graceful. They left no footprints and shadows when they walked. They were beautiful, cheerful and were skilled in communication. One day, they accompanied King Zhao to visit the Yangtze River and the Han River but unfotunately fell into the river and were dead. People came to the river, saw two women who accompanied King Zhao were playing on the riverside ten years later. People built the memorial temple on the riverside to commemorate these two girls. They packed fruits with Dendrobium

早在先秦时期，人们就有春季到河边清洁身体，祛除垢疢的习惯。《太平广记》记载，周昭王登基二十年时，越族献来两位女子，一个叫延娟，一个叫延娱，她们身体轻盈，走路不留脚印，也没有影子，美丽开朗，能言善辩。有一天她们陪昭王游览长江和汉水，不幸落水而亡。十年之后人们又再江边看到有两位女子陪昭王出游，嬉戏于水边。人们在江边修建祠堂纪念这两位姑娘，并用杜兰叶将水果等包好，有的还用五色线包装好沉入水中，免得蛟龙伤害她们的仙体。所以这一天又与死而复苏的生命力有关。

汉代将这一天定为节日，"是月上巳，官民皆絜（洁）于东流水上，曰洗濯祓除，去宿垢疢（病），为大絜"（《后汉书·礼仪志上》）。晚上，家家户户在自己家里每个房间放鞭炮炸鬼，传说这天鬼魂到处出没。曹魏以后把这一天固定下来，叫做"上巳"，而且还增加了水边宴客、郊外踏青玩秋千等内容。临水宴客又被称

nobile leaves, and some of them were packed with five-colored lines and were sank into water lest the flood dragon hurt their fairy bodies. Therefore, this day was related to revival of vitality.

The Han Dynasty used this day as the festival, "It was the Shangsi Festival, when officials and common people cleaned themselves in the eastward water, and cleaning bodies and getting rid of dust (diseases) were called as the great cleaning" (*Book of the Later Han: On Etiquette I*). In the evening, households set off firecrackers to drive away ghosts in each house, because it was said that ghosts appeared everywhere on this day. After the Cao Wei period, this day was fixed and was called "Shangsi", and more contents were included, such as entertaining guests on riverside, having an outing in spring and playing on swings in suburbs and so on. Entertaining guests on riverside was also called

"Floating Goblets", which meant putting goblets with wine in rivers or streams and letting them floating down water; when it stayed in front of somebody, he or she took it from water and drank it. *Records of Jinchu Seasons* wrote that "people came to rivers and ponds and drank wine in floating goblets in winding water on March 3rd." After the Wei and Jin Dynasties, winding water and floating goblets were the main activity on Shangsi Day. "It is Shangsi Day in spring, peach flowers fall in rivers. They don't come back with waves, but flow down rivers. They come onto banks when it rains, and flower goblets turn around..." (Xiaogang, Emperor Jianwen of the Liang Dynasty, *Joint-Sentence Poem on Winding Water*) "The late spring is so beautiful that peach and plum flowers flow in garden. It's just in the season. It's Shangsi Day. Some people visit the Yi and Luo Rivers, and some people come to the Zhen and Wei Rivers… " (Shubao, the last emperor of Chen, *Writing Poems with Ten Rhyming Sentences in the Private Feast on March 3rd in Spring*)

Shangsi is related to feast, entertainment, traveling and recreation, and people spend this day in a happy and festival atmosphere, but March 3rd is related to sad love stories in some places. There is a popular story about a young woman who died for love on Funiu Mountain in Henan:

为 "流觞"，就是将盛有酒水的酒杯放在河水或溪水中，任其顺水而下，当它停留在某人面前时，该人就把酒杯从水中取出来饮之。《荆楚岁时记》："三月三日，士民并出江渚池沼间，为流杯曲水之饮。"自魏晋后，曲水流觞成为上巳日的主要活动。"春色明上巳，桃花落绕沟。波回反不进，给下钩时留。绛水时回岸，花觞转更周……"（梁简文帝萧纲，《曲水联句诗》）"余春尚芳菲，中园飞桃李。是时乃季月。兹日叶上巳。既有游伊洛，可以祓溱洧……"（陈后主叔宝，《春色禊辰尽当曲宴各赋十韵诗》）。

上巳与宴请游乐联系在一起，人们往往在这一天都是在欢乐喜庆的气氛中度过，但是也有一些地方将三月三与悲伤的爱情故事联系在一起。在河南的伏牛山，流传了一个关于殉情姑娘的故事，

伏牛山中有一片竹林，竹林里住着一个美丽的姑娘，人们都叫她贞妹。贞妹爱吹笛子，悠扬好听的笛声一响，各种各样的鸟儿都飞到竹林里，落在竹枝上，听得入了迷。

贞妹的父母相继去世，只留下孤独独的一个姑娘，怎么过生活呢？她想起了石哥。父母在世时把她许给了山上的石哥，她想叫石哥到家里来，商议商议婚事。怎么去说呢？那年夏历三月三，她吹着笛子出了竹林，向山上走去。走到山半腰里，她站了下来，望着峰顶的石哥，不停地吹，悠扬的笛声飘向了山顶，石哥向

There was a bamboo forest in Funiu Mountain, where lived a beautiful girl named Sister Chastity. She loved fluting. Various birds flied into the bamboo forest and stayed on bamboo branches when there was the nice and pleasant fluting, and they were entranced.

The parents of Sister Chastity died one after another, and they left the lonely daughter. How could she live? She thought of Brother Stone. When her parents were still living, they betrothed her to Brother Stone on the mountain, and she wanted to ask him to come to her house to discuss their marriage. How to say to him? She played the flute, came to the bamboo forest and walked towards the mountain. When she came to the halfway up the mountain, she stopped and looked at Brother Stone at the top and continued to flute. The beautiful fluting flowed to the top, and Brother Stone looked down and saw amorous Sister Chastity. He was a stonemason, and made a jade bracelet for Sister Chastity. After it was done, he took it and passed it to shy Sister Chastity. She took the jade bracelet and wore it. They decided that Brother Stone would descend the mountain to marry Sister Chastity on March 3rd next year.

Unfortunately, the king issued an imperial edict that he would choose his concubines from girls under the heaven. The local constable reported the name of Sister Chastity stealthily. One day, several warriors came and caught Sister Chastity. She came to the palace, looked at the jade bracelet and missed her Brother Stone. She wanted to die. Who would live together with Brother Stone until old? Who would cook and make clothes for Brother Stone? She desisted from dying and wanted to grasp a chance to escape from the palace, but she couldn't escape because of the high palace walls and the guarding warriors, which made her feel that meals weren't palatable and tea wasn't sweet. She was worried sick. She stood in the palace yard, looked at rows of southward wild gooses, and made wishes. In the spring, she sang the song, "Wild Goose Door opens on March 3rd, and southward wild gooses will come back soon. They bring letters of Brother stone in rows."

下边一望，看见了多情的贞妹。石哥是一个石匠，他在给贞妹做玉镯，只有一只。玉镯做好了，他拿上玉镯，递给羞答答的贞妹。贞妹接过玉镯戴上了。两个人商议，在来年的三月三，石哥下山去娶贞妹。

谁知，不幸的事儿来了，国王下了诏书，要选天下的姑娘，地保偷偷把贞妹的名字报上了。那天，来了几个武士，把贞妹抓走了。贞妹来到宫里，望着手脖上的玉镯，想念着他的石哥。有心死了吧，将来谁伴石哥白头偕老呢?谁给石哥做饭做衣呢?她打消了死的念头，想瞅机会逃出宫去，宫墙高高的，还有那武士们把着门儿，逃不出去，她吃饭也不香，茶也不甜，简直要把她愁坏了。她站在宫院里，望着南去的一排排大雁，祝愿着。一到春天，她就唱："三月三，雁门升，南去的大雁快回来。一队队一排排，快把哥哥的书信捎回来。"

那年，国王出猎，把贞妹带了出去。猎场上，她一闪身躲避了林子，逃跑了。她翻了一座座山，钻了一层层林，鞋也磨透了，脚也磨烂了，衣裳挂成了一条条，在三月三那天，她摸到了伏牛山里，见到了她的石哥哥。石哥哥却对他呆着脸说："你知道好马不佩双鞍子，一女不配二夫男吗?"

贞妹说："我虽失了身，可我没有失心。"

石哥背过身，不理贞妹。贞妹的心碎了，流着泪离开了石哥。她那两行泪，像清泉一样，流到地上，变成了一条小溪。石哥望着山前的泪溪，知道贞妹的心是贞洁的。他后悔伤了贞妹的心，就顺着泪溪去追贞妹。贞妹听见后边有人追，知道是石哥，可她太伤心了，她头也不回，跑得更快了。她出了伏牛山，再也走不动了，一头栽倒了，变成了一块晶莹的玉石，那玉石越来越大，眨眼变成了一

The king brought Sister Chastity to hunt that year. On the hunting ground, she dodged nimbly, hided herself in the forest and escaped. She climbed many mountains and crossed many forests, with her shoes and feet worn out, her clothes torn into strips. She climbed on Funiu Mountain and saw her Brother Stone on March 3rd. However, Brother Stone gave her a straight face and said to her, "Don't you know that a good horse shall not have two saddles, and a woman shall not have two husbands?"

Sister Chastity answered, "Although I lost my chastity, I have never changed my love."

Brother Stone turned away and didn't answer her. The heart of Sister Chastity was broken, and she left Brother Stone with tears. Her tears flowed on the ground like clear spring and turned into a stream. Brother Stone saw the tear stream in front of the mountain, and knew that the heart of Sister Chastity was pure. He regretted that he had broken the heart of Sister Chastity, and chased her along the tear stream. She heard the chasing of somebody, knew that it was Brother Stone, and she was so sad that she didn't turn back but ran faster. She ran out of Funiu Mountain when she could not move any more, she fell down and turned into a piece of clear jade stone, which became bigger and bigger, and was transformed into a jade mountain at a glance.

Brother Stone threw himself on the jade mountain and wept for a while, and returned in tears.

座玉石山。石哥扑到玉石山上哭了一阵，擦着泪回去了。

Brother Stone came to sweep the tomb of Sister Chastity on the jade mountain on March 3rd next year. There was layers of dust on the jade mountain. He swept but could not clean it. He carried a pair of buckets to the tear stream, then he carried buckets of tears and sweat to clean the jade mountain until there was no dust. He carried buckets to clean the jade mountain on March 3rd every year. Later, Brother Stone died and turned into a dragon, which crouched at the origin of the tear stream, mounted clouds and rode mist, and sprayed water to clean dust on the jade mountain on March 3rd each year.

第二年三月三，石哥去玉石山给贞妹祭扫。玉石山上蒙着一层层灰尘，他扫了扫，怎么也扫不净。他找了一对桶，担起泪溪的水，一挑挑，一担担，流着泪，流着汗，给玉石山冲洗着，直洗得没有一点点灰尘。年年三月三，石哥总要担着桶，去给玉石山洗一次。后来，石哥死了，变成一条龙，卧在泪溪的源头，每年三月三，腾云驾雾，喷水给玉石山洗尘。

Afterwards, because of the clean and white water in the tear stream, people called it White River. The jade mountain lied there lonely and didn't connect with Funiu Mountain, so people called it Lonely Mountain. There is a song passed down that, "Cleaning Lonely Mountain on March 3rd, becoame

后来，人们看泪溪的水清清白白，就叫泪溪为白河。玉石山孤孤独独地在那里卧着，不与伏牛山相连，就叫玉石山为独山。每年三月三，总有一团云彩飘到独山，朝独山下着细雨。人们都说那是

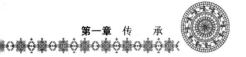

石哥泪洗独山。还传下来一首歌谣："三月三，洗独山，贞妹忠贞心一片，石哥悔泪流万年①。"

Sister Chastity had a pure heart, Brother Stone regretted with tears for ten thousand years."[1]

①雪犁 等主编,《中华民俗源流集成（节日岁时卷）》,甘肃人民出版社,1994年,第166-168页

[1]Collection of Chinese Folk Customs and Sources (Volume of Holidays and Seasons), pp166-168.

3 隋唐时期
The Sui and Tang Dynasties

In the magnificent Sui and Tang Dynasties, "Shangsi" on March 3rd became much more colorful and got more passionate contents. It was an imperial convention, as well as a festival in which common people participated actively. "It's Shangsi Festival in the late spring. The floating goblets make me think of the Orchid Pavilion, and I bear the gold sword and obtain the gold person. The wind is gentle, and the water is green; it's warm, and the flowers are so beautiful. The phenomena of the universe rotate with bright stars, and the imperial way is elaborated. I am respectful, cautious and self-restraint and I keep pure and true. I shall give up traveling and enjoying happiness, so I write the poem and show it to the courtiers." (Li Shi's *Showing the Poem Written on the Third Day to the Courtiers*) In the palace, the party which the emperor entertained the courtiers was so grand, luxurious and splendid, "The two boats are tied with brocades, and the banquet is sumptuous with graceful and solemn music. The

在气势恢宏的隋唐时代，三月三"上巳"有了更多明丽、奔放的内容，它不仅成为宫廷的一个习俗，更是成为民间老百姓纷纷参与其中的节日。"佳节上元巳，芳时属暮春。流觞想兰亭，捧剑得金人。风轻水初绿，日晴花更新，天文信昭回，皇道颇敷陈。恭己每从俭，清心常保真。戒兹游衍乐，书以示群臣。"（李适《三日书怀因示百僚》）。在宫廷里，君王宴请群臣的宴会场面宏大，奢侈豪华，"锦缆方舟渡，琼筵大乐张。风摇垂柳色，花发弄林香。"

（陈希烈《奉和圣制三月三日》）。在宴会上还有歌舞助兴，"画鹢移仟妓，金貂列上公。清歌邀落日，秒舞向春风。"（王维《奉和制上巳于望春亭观禊应制》），"酒筵嫌落絮，舞袖怯春风。"（王维《三月三日勤政楼侍宴应制》），一派欢乐祥和的气氛。

willows are swaying in the wind, and the flowers make the whole forest fragrant." (Chen Xilie's *Responding to the Emperor's March 3rd*) There were songs and dances on the party for fun, "Singing girls are dancing on the boat, and the superior gentlemen are seated with golden mink coat. The fair songs invite the sunset, and the dancers dance in the spring breeze." (Wang Wei's *Responding to the Emperor's Watching the Ceremony in Spring Outlook Pavilion on March 3rd According to His Order*) "There are falling catkins on the wine banquet, and dancing sleeves are waved in the spring breeze." (Wang Wei's *Feast in Diligent Government Building on March 3rd under the Order of the Emperor*), and the atmosphere was so happy and peaceful.

Common people went to outskirts in places with beautiful views and dense grass and forests, especially near lively Qujiang. Boats on the lake were provided to upper class of gentlemen and scholars to appreciate beautiful view of early spring. The poems can be used as proofs. "It's clear on Shangsi Day, and there is a pleasant spring view. The flowers bloom beautifully on the trees and the birds sing fairly on the branches. Luoyang rich men and Chang'an frivolous men go to Qianjin Weir in the east and Yanjing Slope in the west. There are flowing smokes in the sky, and the high willows are drooping gently… " (Shen Xiuwen's *A Poem Written Casually on March 3rd*) "Where has the beautiful deep spring? It's Shangsi in the deep spring. There is a wine party in the Orchid Pavilion, and the flowers bloom on the banks of Quluo. Children paddle in the boats, and women wearing clean coats are in the carriages. A trophy is hung in the place of boating competition." (Bai Juyi's *Responding to Deep Spring in No. 15 of Twenty Poems*) Men of letters grasped the chance to organize poem fairs, where they met with friends and wrote poems, and they were free and sincere, and enjoyed pleasantly, "I set out by ship, and the flowers bloom in the deep spring. I am deeply moved by the beautiful season, and memorize Xunzi's thoughts besides Han River. It's Shangsi in March, and there are the goblets with wine. I sing songs with nobody, and I have no friends to enjoy happiness. The sun sets in the north of the Orchid Pavilion, and there are smokes besides Qu River. The beautiful maids select silkworms

在民间，上巳节时老百姓纷纷到郊外风景秀美、花草繁茂的地方游玩，尤其热闹非凡的曲江一带，湖中备有船只供上层仕族文人登舟欣赏初春的美景。有诗为证，"丽日属元巳，年芳具在斯。开花巳匝树，流嘤复满枝。洛阳繁华子，长安轻薄儿。东出千金堰，西临雁惊坡。游丝映空转，高扬拂地重。"（沈休文《三月三日率尔成篇》），"何处春深好，春深上巳家。兰亭席上酒，曲洛岸边花。弄水游童棹，湔裙小妇车。齐桡争渡处，一匹锦标斜。"（白居易《和春深二十首之十五》）。文人墨客也纷纷趁此机会组织诗会，以诗会友，自由率真，尽情享乐，"摇艇侯明发，花源弄晚春。在山怀绮季，临汉忆荀陈。上巳期三月，浮杯与十旬。坐歌空有待，行乐恨无邻。日晚兰亭北，烟开曲水滨。浴蚕逢姹女，采艾值幽人。古壁堪题序，沙场好解神。群公望不至，虚掷此芳晨。"（孟浩然，《上巳日涧南园期王山人陈七诸公不至》）。

by soaking and cleaning and the hermits pluck mugwort. I write poems on the ancient wall and I am lost in the wild thoughts of battlefield. All the gentlemen don't come, and it's such a pity that the beautiful view is wasted."(Meng Haoran's *Waiting for All the Gentlemen including Wang Shanren and Chen Qi Not Coming to Jiannan Garden on Shangsi*)

三月三日与乐天及河南李尹奉陪裴令公泛洛禊

Accompanying Duke Pei with Letian and the Governor Li of Henan for Xiuqi in Luo River on March 3rd.

【唐】刘禹锡

[The Tang Dynasty] Liu Yuxi

洛下今修禊，群贤胜会稽。

盛筵陪玉铉，通籍尽金闺。

波上神仙妓，岸傍桃李蹊。

水嬉如鹭振，歌响杂莺啼。

历览风光好，沿洄意思迷。

棹歌能俪曲，墨客竞分题。

It's the day of Xiuqi in Luo River, where all the gentlemen get together. I accompany the superior courtiers in the grand feast, and they are the officials in the court.

Fairy dancers dance on the waves and people are attracted on the banks. Water games are like flying egrets and songs are like music of birds.

The view is so beautiful that I lose my thoughts along the stream. Boating songs are pleasant, and men of letters write poems.

The green veiling links with the clouds and there are fragrant carriages on the streets. People praise moveable brocade screens and horses value brocade saddles which avoid mud.

There is dust outside the palace walls, and the

sun sets in the west of the exuberant forest. The boat is shaped as an aquatic bird, and the shadow of the bridge is as low as the rainbow.

The mountain color is clear and far, and the whistling crow wants to habitat in the evening. Only the companions going spring outing wait for the moon on King Wei's Dam.

Besides going outing in spring and boating on Qu River, Shangsi Festival in the Tang Dynasty added many other contents, such as boating competition, flower appreciation, Qujiang Feast etc. The scene of boating competition was rather violent, which Xue Feng described in *Watching Boating Competition*, "It is clear on the March 3rd, and poplar flowers are around the river and birds sing… Drums are struck for three times when red flags are shaken, and two dragons leap out of water…People besides the river shout loudly, bamboos are hung with colorful ribbons and there is a rainbow. The first boat takes the lead in winning the trophy; the following boat loses advantage although boatmen wave oars. Friends of the losers are so worried and they argue violently. They only regard trophy as winning award, and boats come and go between two banks…"

翠幄连云起，香车向道齐。

人夸绫步障，马惜锦障泥。

尘暗宫墙外，霞明苑树西。

舟形随鹢转，桥影与虹低。

川色晴犹远，乌声暮欲栖。

唯馀踏青伴，待月魏王堤。

除了郊外踏青、曲水泛舟以外，唐代的上巳节还增加了很多其他的内容，例如竞渡、赏花、曲江宴等。竞渡的场面一度相当激烈，就像薛逢的《观竞渡》所描写的那样，"三月三日天清明，杨花绕江啼晓莺。……鼓声三下红旗开，两龙跃出浮水来。……江上人呼霹雳声，竹头彩挂虹霓晕。州船抢水已得标，后船失势空挥桡。疮眉血首争不定，输岸一朋心似烧。只将标示输赢赏，两岸十舟五来往。"

居住在长安的文人们还结伴去赏牡丹，"澹荡韶光三月中，牡丹偏自占春风。时过宝地寻香径，已见新花采故丛。曲水亭西杏园北，浓芳深院红霞色。擢秀全胜珠树林，结根幸在春莲城。艳蕊鲜房次第开，含烟洗露照苍苔。庞眉依林禅僧起，轻翅萦枝舞蝶来。独坐南台时共美，闲行古刹情何已。花间一曲奏阳春，应为芬芳比君子。"（权德光《和李中丞慈恩寺清上人院牡丹花歌》）。

Men of letters living in Chang'an went together to appreciate peonies, "The wind is gentle and the spring fills the air with warmth in March. I come to Ci'en Temple to look for the beauty. Peony is full of spirit and attractive, and shows their new faces on the old branches. The treasure place is near Apricot Orchard to the south and overlooks Qu River to the east. Peonies bloom in the deep yard and shine with a red glow. You take the root in the world of Buddhism, and are more prosperous and fragrant than the treasured trees in the fairy land. Peonies contain clear dew and dense mist, and they compete for beauty and stand together. The master holds the stick and leads the monks to appreciate, and the light-footed colorful butterflies fly abound the flower branches. Zhòngcheng had a beautiful time in the imperial official platform. He snatched a moment of leisure to come to the Buddhist temple. He was so passionate that he wrote Song of Peonies, which was a good poem, and it saw fragrance as a gentleman in the world." (Quan Deguang's *Responding to the Poem of Li Zhongcheng's Song of Peonies of Qingshangren Yard of Ci'en Temple*)

Qujiang Feast was the party to celebrate for new successful scholars in the highest imperial examinations, because the notification date of new successful scholars was just before Shangsi Festival, so people held feasts to celebrate, integrated with going for an outing with floating goblets. They traveled on gaily-painted pleasure boat and were extremely proud of their success, "I travel after passing the imperial examination in spring, and the feast is held in Apricot Garden besides Qujiang River. A poem is written by a purple brush on the pink wall of the fairy land, and the imperial building is under the green willow and is full of the fluting. The bank afar is bright with a beautiful view; the mountains are like emerald in the evening and there is an oasis. I am drunk among the flowers when I return, and there are beautiful vehicles on the luxurious streets like flowing water." (Liu Cang's *Feast in Qujiang after Passing the Imperial Examination*)

曲江宴是为了祝贺新科进士所举办的宴会，因为新科进士的放榜之日恰好在上巳之前，所以在这一天，人们举办筵席祝贺一番，还将郊游、流觞结合起来，乘画舫游玩，春风得意，"及第新春选胜游，杏园初宴曲江头。紫毫粉壁题仙籍，柳色箫声拂御楼。霁景露光明远岸，晚空山翠坠芳洲。归时不省花间醉，绮陌香车似水流。"（刘沧《及第后宴曲江》）。

所以在唐代，上巳成了百姓们欢庆的节日，在觥筹交错、歌舞升平中享受太平盛世的欢愉，通过形式多样的游春活动来表达热情与活力。

Therefore, Shangsi had become the festival of common people for celebration in the Tang Dynasty. They enjoyed time of peace and prosperity in goblets, songs and dances, and various kinds of activities of spring outing expressed enthusiasm and vitality.

4 宋元时期
The Song and Yuan Dynasties

Because the dates of Shangsi Festival, Tomb-Sweeping Festival and Cold Food Festival are almost coincident, so these three festivals have been combined into one festival since the Tang Dynasty. People used peach water in March to clean off bad luck form body and bring good luck and there was a nice story in *Records of Searching for Spirits:*

Long long ago, there was a diligent and pure young man named Lu Chong. He came to the mountain for hunting. He shot a deer with an arrow, but it ran after being shot, so he chased after it for a while. Then it disappeared without a trace, and he

因为上巳节与清明节、寒食节的时间几乎是重合的，因而，唐以后的上巳节其实已经与清明节、寒食节三节合一了。以三月桃花水洗掉身上的晦气，以图吉利，《续搜神记》也有这样一个动人的故事：

从前，有一个勤劳朴实、名叫卢充的青年上山打猎，一箭射中了一只小鹿，小鹿中箭奔跑，卢充紧迫不舍，追了一程，小鹿不知去向，忽见一座清堂瓦舍的府第出现在面前。门前书有"崔府"二字，卢充正在疑惑，从门内走出来一个满面春风的仆人，客客气气地把他请进府去，进去一看，只见香烛摆上，一个如花似玉的姑娘正在等他拜堂。卢充欣然应亲，婚后夫妻恩爱，情投意合。他在此住了三天，仆人即用车把他送回家。卢充思念崔女，好不容易熬过四年。这年三月三日，春光明媚，流水欢湍，卢充在河中洗澡。恍惚间，只见一驾牛车远远而来，车上坐着一个抱娃娃的少妇。进前一看，原来正是他日夜思盼的崔女和他未见面的儿子。卢充喜出望外，夫妻情深意切共叙衷肠……"①

saw a mansion with clean hall and tiles. There were two characters "Cui's Mansion" in the front gate. One agreeable servant came out from the gate and invited him to come into the mansion gently. When he came into it, he saw joss sticks and candles which had been placed, and a beautiful girl was waiting for him to perform the formal wedding ceremony. Lu Chong was pleased to accept the wedding, and the couple loved each other and agreed in opinion after the marriage. He lived there for three days, and the servant sent him home by cart. He missed Cui's daughter, and spent four years uneasily. It was March 3rd that year, which was a bright and beautiful day in spring, and water was flowing happily. Lu Chong bathed in the river. Suddenly, he saw an ox cart coming afar, and a young woman carrying a child sat in it. He saw her when it approached, and they were just Cui's daughter whom he missed day and night and his son whom he had never seen. Lu Chong was so happy, and the couple chatted with each other affectionately..." ①

①李玉川，《中国风土趣话》，世界知识出版社，1988年，第15页

①Funny Stories about Chinese Folk Customs, p15.

This day was also regarded as the birthday of the North Pole Divine of Protecting True Gentleman. Meeting God Race was held on this day in different places. *Mengliang Chronicles* wrote that, "Scholars and common people burn incense and get together in halls. Sacrifice ceremonies are held in all halls and buildings. They pray for national peace and harmony of people. The armies and palace warriors serve the incense burners, who protect the society, guard the platforms and pavilions, stand besides the streets, and the audience watch the views."

In Guanzhong area of Shaanxi, people go outing together on March 3rd of the Xia Calendar and call this activity "Fairy Fair". There was a fairy tale about its origin.

It was said that heavenly peaches were ripe in the heavenly palace on March 3rd. All gods came to take part in the heavenly peach feast and discussed great events in the world.

宋时又以这天为北极佑圣真君的诞辰。各地于这天举行迎神赛会。《梦梁录》云："土庶烧香，分集殿庭。诸宫道宇，俱设醮事，上祈国泰，下保民安。诸军寨及殿司卫奉侍香火者，皆安排社会，结缚台阁，迎列于道，观睹纷纷。"

陕西关中地区，每逢夏历三门初三，人们都要结伴郊游，并把这个活动称做"仙人会"。说起它的来历，还有个神话故事。

传说三月三这天，天宫里的蟠桃熟了。这一天各路神仙都要去赴蟠桃盛会，商谈天上人间大事。

有一次，各路神仙入席后，一面品尝千年仙桃，一面听玉皇大帝说道："诸位分管人间，都要爱民如子，扶助凡人，今天你们就说说人间的事儿吧。"

居住在南方的神仙说："玉帝在上，我们那儿多种稻子，每年雨水太少，稻米歉收，不能为你老奉供，请主体谅。"北方的神仙说："小神所管北方雨水太多，河里常常盛不下，大水淹没了良田和村庄……"玉皇大帝闻奏，就派遣孙悟空前去察看。

孙悟空出了南天门，一个跟斗就翻到了海南岛。但不凑巧，却把他的猴头碰在了山上的石头上。他气愤地说："真是南方旱，地和石头一样硬，不是我老孙头上有功夫，准要碰个头破血流。"于是，又一个跟头，翻回南天门，急忙向玉帝禀报说："玉帝大人，南方就是缺水，我虽没见稻田，可地硬的和石

Once upon a time, when all gods tasted fairy peaches which had been ripe for several thousand years after being seated, the Jade Emperor said to them, "You manage the world and shall love people like your sons and help common people. Please talk about events on the earth today!"

The immortal who lived in the south said, "The Highest Jade Emperor, our people sow rice, but there is a little rain every year and rice is lacked, so I cannot offer rice to your majesty. I hope that you can forgive me. " The northern immortal said, "There is a lot of rain in the north governed by me, rivers often have floods which inundate good fields and villages… "

After hearing their reports, the Jade Emperor assigned Sun Wukong to investigate the conditions.

When Sun Wukong came out of the Southern Gate of Heaven, he turned a somersault to Hainan Island. Unfortunately, his head ran onto the stone on the mountain. He said angrily, "It's dry in the south indeed. The land is as hard as the stone. If I don't have Kung Fu on my head, I must have my head broken." Then, he turned another somersault back to the Southern Gate of Heaven, and reported to the Jade Emperor in a hurry, "the Great Jade Emperor, water was lacked in the south. I didn't see any rice fields, but the land was hard as the stone. Look, my head was almost broken, and it is still swollen!"

After hearing his words, the Jade Emperor let Sun Wukong go to the north to have a look.

Wukong turned another somersault on the earth. Unluckily, he fell into the Yellow River. He kicked his feet, leaped onto a colorful cloud, and said without looking back, "There is too much water in the north, and the water flooded up to my neck even before I stand on the ground." He reported to the Jade Emperor hastily, "I'm afraid that water in the north can drown people. I fell into water when I was on the earth, and even didn't touch the bottom!"

After hearing his words, the Jade Emperor said to Wind Grandmother and Rain Master, "Listen, you shall make less rain in the north but make more rain in the south hereafter."

Since the imperial edict of the Jade Emperor, there have been more rain and wind in the south, and there have been less rain and wind in the north till now.

Sun Wukong came and went to the earth for several times and didn't eat heavenly peaches in the

头差不多。你看，差点把我的头碰破了，这还肿着哪!"

玉帝听了，又让孙悟空再到北方去看看。

悟空又一个跟头翻到了人间。可是不妙，这一回一下栽到黄河里了。只见他脚一蹬，就纵身踏上了彩云，头也不回地说，"北方水就是太多了，我还没沾地，水就淹上了脖子。"他急忙又向玉帝禀报说："不好了，北方的水能把人淹死，我一入凡间就掉入了水中，连底也投探着呢!"

玉帝听后就对风婆和雨师道："你等听着，以后要向北方少雨，对南方多行雨。"

当初玉皇大帝有旨，因此直到如今，南方水多天捞，风多。北方雨少天旱，风少。

话说三月三的神仙会上，只苦了孙悟空一个

人，他往返了几次人间没有吃上蟠桃，玉帝安慰他说："等人间桃子熟了，你就多吃一些吧。"所以至今，猴儿们都喜欢吃桃子。

后来，人们为了让孙悟空如实地向玉帝回报人间实情，便在三月三这天做一种形状如同桃子的花馍供献起来。

关中每到三月三这一天，人们还要把屋里屋外打扫得干干净净，然后三三两两结伴到村外游玩，便把这种郊游称为"仙人会"，也叫"神仙会"。①

除了外出郊游之外，还有地方的人们采集荠菜花带回家，据宋赞宁《物类相感志》云："三月三日收荠菜花，置灯颈上，则飞蛾蚊虫不投。"明田

immortal fair on March 3rd, and the Jade Emperor comforted him, "You can eat more peaches when they are ripe on the earth." Therefore, monkeys like eating peaches till now.

Hereafter, people made flower cakes shaped like peaches to offer to Sun Wukong on March 3rd so that he could report the actual condition on the earth to the Jade Emperor.

On March 3rd, Guanzhong people clean their houses indoors and outdoors, and go sightseeing outside villages in groups, and they call this kind of sightseeing "Fairy Fair" as well as "Immortal Fair".①

Besides going outing, people in some places pick up flowers of shepherd's purse and bring them home. According to Song Zanning's *Record of Interaction of Objects*, "If flowers of shepherd's purse are picked up to be placed on lamp neck, moths and mosquitoes will not put themselves

①雪犁 等主编，《中华民俗源流集成（节日岁时卷）》，甘肃人民出版社，1994年，第164—165页

①Collection of Chinese Folk Customs and Sources (Volume of Holidays and Seasons), pp164—165.

into lamp." *West Lake Sight-Seeing Record of* Tian Rucheng in the Ming Dynasty reads that "men and women wore flowers of shepherd's purse on March 3rd."

汝成《西湖游览志》云："三月三日，男女皆戴荠菜花。"

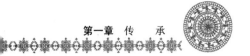

少数民族
Ethnic Minorities

少数民族为什么要过三月三，到底三月三是汉地文化传播到边疆还是其他原因暂且不论，少数民族的三月三节日往往更多涉及文化的起源以及爱情故事的结晶。例如瑶族的三月三节日就和八角树的起源有关了。

古时候，有个姑娘叫观娅。年纪不大不小，戴包头帕。观娅姑娘聪明美丽，一张脸就像盛开的八角花。她织的布，夏天

It will not be included in the discussion such as why national minorities celebrate March 3rd, or whether March 3rd was spread from Han culture to frontier areas or other reasons. One thing for sure is March 3rd Festival of national minorities are often related to the origin of culture and the fruit of love stories. For example, March 3rd Festival of Yao people was related to the origin of star anise trees:

In ancient times, there was a gril named Guanya. She was in her golden age, and wore a scarf on her head. She was clever and beautiful, and her face was like a blooming star anise flower. Cloths woven by her made people cool in summer and made people warm in winter; flowers embroidered by her made bees fly to gather honey, and butterflies fly around; He singing made thrushes fly down from trees, and carps jump out of rivers…

One day, Guanya hoed up weeds in the indigo land. She was thirsty at noon and came to the stream to drink water. The stream flowed from the large river at the mountain top. There were several little trees with bright yellow leaves among weeds besides the stream, which were so charming. Guanya took the bush-hook from her waist and cut off grass and unspecified trees, loosened the soil for these small trees, and came to make indigo till she hoed up for small trees in the whole forest.

Unexpectedly, these small trees grew up in wind and rain in one or two years. Small red flowers bloomed in March, April, August and September. They had pairs of petals which just numbered eight, Guanya called them star anise trees. If grass and trees in the world bloom, they must bear fruits. The star anise trees bloomed red and fragrant flowers, but didn't bear one star anise fruit.

穿了使人凉爽，冬天穿了使人暖和，她绣的花，蜜蜂飞来采蜜，蝴蝶飞来打转，她唱的歌，画眉听了飞下树，鲤鱼听了跳出水……

一天，观娅在蓝靛地里锄草。到了晌午，她口渴了，就到小溪边喝水。这条小溪，是从山顶上的大菁里流下来的。小溪边的杂草丛中长着稀稀疏疏的小树，树上嫩黄鲜亮的叶子，非常逗人喜爱。观娅就取下腰间别着的钩刀，砍掉了草和杂树，还为那些小树松了土，直到把整片小树林锄完，才又去蓝靛。

没想到才一两年，那些小树顶风冒雨长高了。三四月和八九月间，还要开红色的小花呢。那花瓣，双双对对，不多不少，刚好八瓣，观娅就给它取名叫八角树。世间草木，开花必结果。八角树开的花，红艳艳，香喷喷的，但一个八角果果也结不出来。

有一年夏历三月三日，观娅薅锄过的八角树又开花了，大朵小朵的，红得像彩云一般。她走到小溪边，爬上八角树，摘下一朵八角花，忧伤地唱道：

绿叶绿树绿枝桠，

枝枝桠桠开红花。

只见开花不结果，

何时结果才开花?

她唱完，叹了口气，把那朵八角花向空中抛去。那朵花随风在她头上旋转了几下，便飞下斜坡，飞过小溪，飘落在对面一片开着白色小花的树林中，贴在一个小伙子的胸前。

观娅顺着八角花飞去的方向一看，才看见对面小溪边也有一片小树林，每棵树都开着白生生的小花，有一个小伙子正站在花树上。她一见到那漂亮

It was March 3rd in the traditional Chinese Calendar one year, the star anise trees which Guanya hoed up bloomed and the big and small flowers were as red as colorful clouds. She walked to the stream, climbed one star anise tree, plucked a star anise flower and sang sadly:

Green leaves, trees and branches!

They bloom red flowers.

They bloom but don't bear fruits,

When will they bear fruits after blooming?

After singing the song, she sighed and threw the star anise flower into the sky. The flower rotated on her head with wind, flew down the slope, over the stream, fell into the forest with the small white flowers on the opposite, and stuck on the breast of a young fellow.

Looking at the direction which the star anise flower flew, she saw a forest of small trees besides the stream, each tree with the small white flowers, and a young fellow standing on a flower tree. When she saw the handsome young man, her face became red at once. The young fellow on the flower tree on the opposite was named Dali, who had worn the head scarf just for several years, and was strong and kind. He was skilled in hunting. When he met a tiger, he could jump on its back, break its head; when he met an eagle, he could bent a bow and nock an arrow, and shoot its eye with an arrow. Therefore, his name was popular, and was spread to Guanya's ears.

Dali looked at the star anise flower stuck on his breast, then at Guanya who was as beautiful as a fairy. Plucked a small white flower and threw it to her.

The small white flower rotated and flew like a white butterfly. It flew over the stream, and fell into the hand of Guanya. Before she had time to see the flower, she heard Dali singing:

Green leaves, trees and branches!

They bloom white flowers.

 Red flowers, white flowers and star anise flowers,

They bear fruits and become one family.

的小伙子，脸马上红了。对面花树上的小伙子叫达利，刚包头帕不几年，身强力壮，心地善良。他打猎的本领很高，碰到老虎，他可以跳上虎背，砸烂老虎的头，遇到飞鹰，他弯弓搭箭，可以一箭射中它的眼睛。为此，达利的名字越传越远，也传到了观娅的耳朵里。

达利看了看胸前沾着的八角花，又看了看观娅，见她长得像天仙一般，便摘了一朵白色小花，向观娅抛过来。

那朵小白花，像只白蝴蝶，飞着飞着，飞过小溪，落到观娅手巾。观娅还没来得及看花，就听见达利唱道：

绿叶绿树绿枝桠，

枝枝枉枉开白花。

红花白花八角花，

结了果果成一家。

观娅脸红了，心跳了。她低头看那朵白花，同她抛去的红花一样大小，一样芳香，一样有八瓣。她抬头仔细看对面的小树，叶子一样的形状，一样的颜色。她就笑着把小白花簪在头上，笑眯眯地又唱道：

白花红花一种花，

八片花瓣一样大。

同齐栽来同齐长，

同条小溪来开花。

达利听了，心头甜蜜蜜的，赶紧接着唱：

红花白花八角花。

不结八角不成家。

观娅听到这里，乐了，也接唱道：

八角哪月结了果，

Guanya's face turned red and her heartbeat was quickened. She lowered her head to look at the white flower, which was as big and fragrant as the red flower thrown by her, and had eight petals too. She raised her head to observe the small trees on the opposite carefully, and found their leaves and colors were the same. She stuck the small white flower into her hair with a smile, and sang cheerily:

Red flowers and white flowers are the same,

Their eight petals have the same size.

They are planted and grow up at the same time,

They bloom besides the same stream.

After hearing her song, Dali felt sweet and sang hastily:

Red flowers, white flowers and star anise flowers,

They will not have family until they bear star anise fruits.

After hearing his song, Guanya was pleased, and she continued to sing:

When will star anise trees bear fruits?

When will the two persons become a couple?

In this way, they sang songs and threw flowers continuously. Red star anise flowers flew over the stream like red butterflies in groups; white star anise flowers flew over it in groups like white butterflies. A few of them fell on their bodies, and most of them fell on the star anise trees. They sang songs from dawn to sundown, and they became more enthusiastic when they sang more songs. When the sun set, they parted with reluctance and came home.

Strangely, the former star anise flowers which didn't bear fruits began to bear fruits hereafter. Between August and September, either trees of red star anise flowers or those of white star anise flowers on both banks of the stream bore bunches of fragrant star anise fruits. Branches were bent down by them, and both banks of the stream were covered with them.

When the banks of the stream were filled with star anise flowers on March 3rd of the Xia Calendar next year, Guanya and Dali married. In the morning, Guanya used red, white, yellow and blue cloths to make flower bags according to the shape of star anise, and put six cereals into them, each point tied with spikes, and she led girls and lads to throw bags at each other and sing love songs in antiphonal style.

哪月两人来成家。

这样，她俩不断地唱歌，不断地抛花，小溪上空，红八角花像红蝴蝶，成群结队地飞过去，白八角花像白蝴蝶，成群结队地飞过来，小部分落在他俩身上，大部分落在八角树上。他俩从早唱到晚，越唱越多，越唱心越热。太阳快落坡时，才依依不舍地离别回家去。

说来也怪，以前的八角花不会结果，从那以后，就结果了。八九月间，小溪两岸，不管红八角花，白八角花，都结满了八角，一串又一串，香喷喷的，压弯了树枝，盖满了小溪两岸。

第二年夏历三月三日，小溪两岸开满八角花的时候，观娅和达利成亲了。当天早晨，观娅用红、白、黄，蓝四色布，仿照八角模样缝成花包，装上六谷，并在每个角上拴上花穗，带着姑娘和小伙子们互相抛掷，对唱情歌。晚上又在家里杀鸡杀鸭，款待寨中三亲六戚。就这样，一直延续了三天三夜。观娅和达利成亲后，他们教乡亲们把会结果的八角栽到山山岭岭、村村寨寨。八角树好比摇钱树，几年，瑶家就富裕起来。不知过了多少年，在一年的三月三日，观娅和达利一同归世。为了纪念观娅和达利为瑶族培育八角，歌颂观娅和达利之间纯真的爱情，每年夏历三月三日，姑娘小伙子们都一群一群的到山上八角林中丢花包、唱情歌，到了晚上又回到家杀鸡杀鸭祭献。这风习一代传一代，成了瑶家最隆重的传统节日①。

In the evening, they killed chickens and ducks to entertain relatives in villages. The celebration lasted three days and three nights. After Guanya and Dali married, they taught villagers to plant star anise trees on mountains and in villages. Star anise trees were like money trees, and Yao people became rich after a few years. Guanya and Dali died together on March 3rd one year. In order to memorize Guanya and Dali who cultivated star anise for Yao people and praise the pure love between Guanya and Dali, young women and men come to star anise forests on mountains to throw flower bags and sing love songs, and kill chickens and ducks for sacrifice in the evening on March 3rd of the Xia Calendar every year. The custom has been passed from generation to generation and has become the grandest festival of Yao people.[1]

①雪犁 等主编，《中华民俗源流集成（节日岁时卷）》，甘肃人民出版社，1994年，第158-161页

①Collection of Chinese Folk Customs and Sources (Volume of Holidays and Seasons), pp158-161.

As for Miao people in West Hunan, the March 3rd of lunar calendar is the festival which they sing songs and dance in festival attires. This festival was hard-earned.

It was said that there were timely wind and rain in ancient times, so they ate and wore well and Miao people were pleased.

Once a time, young people in Bajiao Village and Langmu Village fought for a pretty "Daipa" (girl). As a result, people of both villages were hurt and one man from Langmu Village was killed. Both villages became feuds hereafter, and no one dared to go to the other village.

Afterwards, people of Langmu Village carried coffins and ghosts to prepare for fighting, and all people in the village came to assist in fighting. They took broadswords, spears and choppers, climbed two mountains, came to the border of Luxi County, and saw large Bajiao Village of high topographical relief. Langmu Village sent here a lot of people and horses which meant that something must happen. Bajiao Village gathered all people and horses together in a short time and tented on the opposite mountain, and both villages didn't dare to infringe upon the other.

对于湖南湘西的苗族来说，农历三月初三是他们穿节日盛装在一起唱歌跳舞的节日。这一个节日来之不易呢。

相传，古时候风调雨顺，人们吃得饱穿得好，苗家的男女老少都高兴。

有一次，芭蕉坪和郎木坪的男女青年为了争夺一个年轻好看的"黛帕"（姑娘）打起来了，结果双方都有人受伤，郎木坪的一位青年还被打死了。从此两边就结下了怨仇，谁也不敢到对方的寨子里伸脚。

后来，郎木坪的人们抬棺抬鬼准备再战，全村寨的男男女女，老老少少都去助战。他们拿起大刀梭镖和柴刀翻过两重山，来到泸溪县边界。芭蕉坪寨子大，地势高，看到郎木坪寨的大队人马众多，一定有事，于是在很短的时间内也集合了所有人马，在对面山上扎营，双方谁也不敢侵犯对方。由

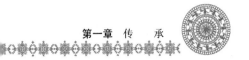

于人多马众，热闹得很，人们从来没经过这样聚居的生活，就把仇恨忘掉了，在山上摆起大大的歌场和舞场，大家尽情地唱了一天一夜，也尽情地跳了一天一夜，直到天明才难分难舍地各自回家了。这天，正是三月初三。第二年有一个叫南山坎九娘的，她邀请了许多男女青年，在三月初三的那天穿起美丽的衣服，戴起好看的花帕子，从村寨里跳呀唱呀的一直跑到去年歌舞的那个山顶上。有很多年轻小伙子也穿上最漂亮的衣裳跟去了，陪那些姑娘们唱歌跳舞。这时候正是百花盛开的季节，山上的良辰美景使青年男女触景生情，有说不完的话，唱不完的歌，直到天黑还舍不得回家①。后来，苗族同胞就三月三定为"龙花会"。

Because there were so many bustling people and horses, and people had never lived together, they forgot their hatred and prepared for large singing stage and dancing stage. They sang a day and night happily, danced a day and night passionately, parted with reluctance and returned home until the dawn. It was just March 3rd. A young woman named the Ninth Aunt Nanshankan invited many young women and men to dance and sing from the village. They ran to the top of the mountain where they sang and danced last year with pretty clothes and nice colorful scarves on March 3rd. It was the season of one hundred flowers in full bloom. The beautiful views on the mountain attracted young men and women, and they talked and sang songs endlessly and were reluctant to go home①. Hereafter, Miao people fixed March 3rd as "Dragon Flower Fair".

①雪犁 等主编，《中华民俗源流集成（节日岁时卷）》，甘肃人民出版社，1994年，第172—173页

①Collection of Chinese Folk Customs and Sources (Volume of Holidays and Seasons), pp172–173.

第二章

流　布

　　三月三来三月三，婆婆们去爬云门山。云门山上有神仙，神仙身边有仙丹。吃了仙丹好了病，年年忘不了那三月三。

——青州苏闻乡阎河村民歌

　　走过千年岁月的中华民族，是如此的精彩。善良的人民用自己勤劳的双手在这片土地上创造了灿烂辉煌的中华文明，也将文化的火种传送到四面八方。三月三这样一个民俗节日，也逐渐在中华大地上传播开来。无论是为了祭祖、崇神、驱邪、避鬼，还是为了祈求平安、家和人兴，全国各地的老百姓以各种形式庆祝三月三，张灯结彩，喜气洋洋，为中华文化增加了更多内容，这种多样性的分布，也是民俗文化的魅力所在。

Chapter Two

Circulation

Old women climb Yunmen Mountain on March 3rd. There are immortals with divine pills on Yunmen Mountain. Their diseases will be cured if they eat divine pills, so they cannot forget March 3rd each year.

——Villagers' Song of Yanhe, Suwen Village, Qingzhou

China has a wonderful history of several thousand years. Kind-hearted people created the splendid and brilliant Chinese civilization on this land with their diligent hands, and passed the cultural fire everywhere. March 3rd has been spread as a folk festival in China. Common people in China celebrate March 3rd in different forms in order to sacrifice to ancestors, worship gods, drive out evil spirits, ward off ghosts as well as pray for peace, harmonious family and prosperity, they hang up lanterns and festoons, are raptured and add more contents to Chinese culture, and this diversification is the charm of folk culture.

1

河洛中原
Heluo Central Plain

In order to commemorate Fuxi and Nüwa, common people in Henan go to market, buy vegetable and flower seeds to sow on March 3rd. It's said that seeding on this day can obtain richer and better harvest, "Going to North Pass on March 3rd, you can have many pumpkins and bottle gourds." Moreover, they dig shepherd's purse and bring it home, eat it with eggs, which can build a sound body. In Xinxian County and Guangshan County, local people had the convention of avoiding ghost and evil spirits on March 3rd before the liberation, it was said that it was the day for the Hell to grasp people, so households set off firecrackers to ward off evil spirits and ghosts and pray for peace. Several heads of garlic were placed at gates of households, which meant "forgetting it". When they slept in the evening, their shoes were placed upside down in front of beds, which made ghosts coming to grasp people think that no one was at home. More

无论是纪念伏羲还是女娲，河南的老百姓在三月初三这一天会去赶集买菜籽、花籽等下种，因为据说这一天播种下去，收获会格外丰富一些，收成也好一些，"三月三，上北关，南瓜葫芦结一千"。另外就是挖荠菜带回家，与鸡蛋一起吃，可以强身健体。在新县、光山一带，新中国成立前当地人民在三月三都有防鬼避邪的习俗，据说这一天是阴曹地府抓人的日子，所以家家户户要在晚上燃放鞭炮，驱邪逐鬼，以求平安。各家门口还要放几颗大蒜，即"算了吧"。晚上睡觉时，脱在床前的鞋子也要倒着摆放，让前来抓人的小鬼们认为家里没有人。有些胆子比较大的人，半夜的时候还到野外去看"鬼火"，俗称"看灯"①。

在方城县东北50余里的黄石山，当地群众在三月三的时候会去黄石山拜祖师爷。黄石山俗名小顶山，又名小武当山，每年三月三的时候，人们都要在小顶山举办香火会，相传道教祖师爷真武玄天大帝先在此地修真，后来才搬到大顶山（武当山）。三月三是祖师爷的生日，道教弟子在这一天烧香膜拜祖师爷，后来渐渐成为当地的香火会了。

daring people went in the wild to see "ghost fire" at midnight, which was called "watching lanterns"①.

Huangshi Mountain is located in over 50 *li* to the northeast of Fangcheng County, and local people climb it to worship the venerable masters on March 3rd. The local name of Huangshi Mountain is Small Ding Mountain, which is also called Small Wudang Mountain. People come to hold Incense Ceremony on Small Ding Mountain on March 3rd, and it was said that the Truly Martial Mysterious Heavenly Grand Emperor nourished his true nature here and moved to Large Ding Mountain (Wudang Mountain). March 3rd was the birthday of the venerable master, Taoist disciples went to burn incense and worshiped him on the day, and it became the local incense ceremony gradually. According to the local convention, pilgrims shall climb to the top of the mountain with incense bags on them and yellow flags in their hands, they go into the temple to burn incense, make wishes and fulfill their promises. In order to show sincerity,

---

①甘肃省古籍文献整理编译中心编，《中国民俗知识 河南民俗》，甘肃人民出版社，2008年，95—96页

①Knowledge of Chinese Folk Customs: Henan Folk Customs, ed. by Guansu Collection, Compilation & Translation Center for Ancient Books/ 2008, pp95–96.

people are needled when they arrive at the foot of the mountain. There are two conditions of needling: the first is needling on two cheeks, red flower is hung at one end, steamed bread is pricked at the other end, and people walk with jerky steps and blood drops. The second is needling on both arms, and hands are twisted together. People with needles enter the gate of the temple, they are supported by their companions, kowtow three times in one step and bow three times in three steps. Then they burn incense and kowtow in front of the venerable master, bow and worship, then an old Taoist take down the needles, put incense dust on them, and they walk down the mountain with quick steps when they accomplish their pious deeds.

按照当地的习俗，凡是朝观者，必须身挂香包，手执小黄旗，成群结队，攀登峰巅，进庙烧香，许愿还愿。为表诚意，一踏入山脚即便上针。上针分两种情况1、两腮过针，一端坠红绒花，一端扎蒸馍，一走一颠，鲜血滴滴点点，2、二臂上针，叉手不离方寸。上针的人进入祖师殿门，由同行人搀扶，一步三叩首，三步九搭躬，直至祖师面前，烧香磕头，躬身揖拜，老道将针取下，敷上香灰，功果完满信步下山。

此习俗从明代以来颇为盛行，而明祖朱棣又尤其崇奉祖师，在大小武当山修建庙宇。如今小顶山有六宫十一殿，香火会规模盛大，善男信女们带来的香纸将焚香炉都遮盖满了，庙院里香烟缭绕[①]。

在陕西的汉阴，每年的三月三都有一个"古会"，届时无论是城镇居民还是乡镇村民，都要到集镇来参加这个古会，还有不少花鼓词和山歌咏唱这个古会呢。三月三古会，又叫三月三骡马会，亦称上巳古会，根据当

①王金祥主编，《方城民俗志》，中州古籍出版社，1991年，第333页

The convention has been popular since the Ming Dynasty. Zhu Di, the founder of the Ming Dynasty worshiped the venerable master extremely, and built temples in Large Wudang Mountain and Small Wudang Mountain. There are six palaces and eleven halls on Small Ding Mountain at present, the scale of Incense Ceremony is grand, incense paper brought by devout men and women cover incense burners, and incense smoke curl up in temples[①].

In Hanyin of Shaanxi, there is an "Ancient Fair" on March 3rd every year, township residents and village residents come to towns to participate in this ancient fair, and there are many flower drum lyrics and mountain songs about this ancient fair. March 3rd ancient fair is also called March 3rd Mule and

①Study of Folk Customs of Fangcheng County, ed. by Wang Jinxiang/1991, p333.

Horse Fair as well as Shangsi Fair, and the local inscription records that, "Longgang used March 3rd as Fair of Farm Utensils, farmers assembled here from several hundred *li*, exchanged what one had for what one didn't have and it would be inconvenient without fairs..." On the temple fair on March 3rd, farmers and tradesmen gather together here with commodities such as farm cattle, rake etc. to conduct transactions, and it's said that businessmen from Sichuan, Gansu and Hubei come to participate in temple fair which is lively and extraordinary[①].

In Tianjin, which is a coastal city, people celebrate the birthday of the Goddess of Heaven on March 3rd and hold the Heavenly Peach Fair for celebration. In the past, people came to Small Shaozhikou Eternity Palace to hold celebration activities at over ten *li* in the west of the old city, and Zhaijiao religious activities for three days consecutively. Devout men and women came to burn incense and prayed blessing to celebrate the

①Historical Accounts of Hanyin County, Volume 1, p50.

地的碑文记载，"龙岗旧以三月三日为农器之会，数百里农人集此，以有易无，无庙不便⋯⋯"。在三月三的庙会上，农民、商贩纷纷云集于此，带着耕牛、锄耙等商品来赶会交易，据说连汉中甚至四川、甘肃、湖北的客商都前来参加庙会，一时间热闹非凡[①]。

在海滨城市的天津，人们在三月三这一天要给王母娘娘祝贺寿诞，举办蟠桃会来庆贺。以前，从三月初一开始，人们就会在旧城西10余里处的小稍直口福寿宫举办庆祝活动，连续三天都要举办斋醮活动。届时，善男信女

①陕西省汉阴县政协文史资料委员会主编，《汉阴县文史资料》第一辑，1987年，第50页

们纷纷前来烧香祈福，不论路途远近，来给王母娘娘庆贺。在此期间，福寿宫的道士们还邀请市内知名士绅、大富人家来庙里吃斋念经；在宫外，各个香会还要搭席棚举行设摆，面向公众展出各种古玩家具等等。

Goddess of Heaven regardless of distance. During the period, Taoists in Eternity Palace invited famous gentlemen and rich men in the city to come to the temple to practice abstinence from meat and chant sutras; outside the palace, people of incense fairs built sheds to place and display various kinds of antique furniture to the public.

2 边隆之地
Frontier Land

In the places such as Ninghai and Leqing in Zhejiang, March 3rd is also called Shangsi Festival, people come to riverside to set up pot and stove to burn rice, and think that "heavenly rice is boiled on March 3rd, which can make people clever", they pluck flowers of shepherd's purse to wear on heads, because "people will not have headache if they wear red flowers of shepherd's purse". People in vicinity of Bian Mountain of Changxing come to fields to dig wild shallots, bring them home to eat, think that they can detoxicate and avoid plague and evil spirits. The grandest activities celebrating March 3rd are held in Shaoxing and Wenzhou.

在浙江宁海和乐清等地，三月三也被称为上巳节，人们在这一天除了去水边搭起临时锅灶烧饭吃，认为"三月三，煮天下饭，吃了会聪明"，还采摘荠菜花戴在头上，因为"戴了荠菜红，一年头不痛"。长兴弁山一带的人们到田地里去挖野胡葱，带回家食用，认为它能解毒，辟瘟邪。庆祝三月三的活动，最盛大的莫过于绍兴和温州了。

绍兴人民代代相传，说三月初五为夏禹生日。古时候，尤其是明清时期，每到这一天，皇帝就会来到会稽山下的禹庙，御祭或诰祭大禹。会稽山以禹会诸侯于此，据说大禹在这里去世并葬在此地，后来这里还被封为南镇。每年的三月初五，老百姓就前往禹庙祭拜夏禹并祈求保佑平安。《康熙

Shaoxing people have carried on the saying from generation to generation that the fifth day of the third lunar month was the birthday of Yu, who is the founder of the Xia Dynasty. In ancient times, especially during the Ming and Qing Dynasties, emperors came to Yu's Temple under Kuaiji Mountain, offered an imperial sacrifice or an imperial mandate to Dayu. Yu met feudal princes on Kuaiji Mountain, it was said that Dayu was buried here after his death, and it was invested with Southern Town here. Common people come to Yu's Temple to worship Yu and pray for peace on March 5th every year. *Kuaiji Records of Kang Xi* wrote that, "Yu's Temple was crowded with a large number of tourists on the birthday of Yu. Rich people, superior people and inferior people came out. Gentlemen were in gaily-painted pleasure-boats. There were paint coatings on walls and plenty of wine utensils and tableware. Guests and hosts were seated to appreciate songs and dances. Common people liked showing off, they spent all savings to travel on lakes to enjoy themselves for several days although they weren't rich."

Common people of Wenzhou worship gods differently in early March. In Wenzhou, people worship King of Loyalty and Peace whose popular name was "Marshal Wen", he is the local immortal and grasps local peace. In early March, common

会稽志》记其事云：
"禹生之日，禹庙游人最盛。无论富贵贱，倾城俱出。士民皆乘画舫，丹垩鲜明，酒樽食具甚盛。宾主列坐，前设歌舞。小民尤相矜尚，虽非富饶，亦终岁储蓄，以为下湖之行春，俗尽数日。"

温州老百姓在三月初的祭拜神祇又不相同。在温州，人们崇敬的是忠靖王，俗称"温

元帅"，他是地方神仙，掌管一方平安。每逢三月初，老百姓就抬着忠靖王的神像，请王出庙巡行，以驱瘟疫。忠靖王据说是唐代的一名秀才，"忠靖王姓温名琼，温州平阳人。唐长安二年生，至二十六岁，因举士不第，幻化为神，为民除灾害，于是逐皆祠王，以祈灵响矣"。

还有一则民间传说，讲述忠靖王是怎样成为神仙的。

people carry the image of King of Loyalty and Peace, invite him to go out of the temple to patrol in order to expel plague. It was said that King of Loyalty and Peace was a scholar in the Tang Dynasty, "The name of King of Loyalty and Peace was Wen Qiong, and he came from Pingyang of Wenzhou. He was born in the second year of Chang'an in the Tang Dynasty, he was miraculously transformed into a god because he failed in the imperial examination when he was twenty-six years old, he expelled disasters for people, became the King of Temple in order to pray for spirits."

There is another folklore telling about how King of Loyalty and Peace became an immortal.

It was said that there was a scholar named Wen Qiong in Pingyang County in the Tang Dynasty, he was well-featured and handsome, and he was honest and good and liked to help poor people in normal times. Scholar Wen had bad luck, he came to the capital to take part in the imperial examinations, he failed consecutively, but he continued to study hard and tried to improve himself.

One day, he read till midnight and suddenly heard two people talking gently outside the window. One said coarsely, "Hey, I felt tired for a whole night, but we cannot find the place to start. Forgot it!" Another answered gently, "Do you see the well beside the temple? There are many people to carry water everyday, and I think it's better to put it into the well!"

Wen Qiong opened the door, but couldn't see anyone. He thought over for a moment, and understood that two plague ghosts put poison into the well. He came to the well and guarded it till the dawn. When people from all directions came to the well to carry water, Wen Qiong guarded the well and persuaded them, "The well water was poisonous, and it is better for you to carry water from other places." People didn't believe him and said, "The

相传，在唐代，平阳县有个姓温名琼的秀才，长得五官端正，面目清秀，为人忠厚善良，喜欢帮助穷人。那温秀才时运不佳，进京赴考，连连落第，但仍继续苦读，力图上进。一次，他在温州城内一座庙宇中，租了一间客房，日夜攻读诗书。

一个晚上，他读书到深夜忽然听到窗外有两人在轻轻谈话；一个粗里粗气的声音说："嘿，累了一夜，还找不到下手地方，算了吧！"另一个细声细气的声音回答说："你看见庙旁边这口水井吗？这里每天挑水的人很多，我看就放在这口井中吧！"

温琼关了门出去，却不见人影。他想了一会，悟到这是两个疫鬼在井中放毒。他就去那口水井边，一直守到天亮。这时，挑水的人从四面八方来到井边挑水，温琼一面护住井口，一面劝说大伙儿：

"这井水有毒,你们还是到别处去挑吧!"可是大家不信,说:"这井水又清又冽,我们天天吃,怎么说是有毒呢?"有人还讥笑地说:"这个秀才,读书读糊涂了。"

温琼看说服不了大家,就高高站在井沿上,说:"你们不信,就让我以身试水吧!"他纵身往下一跳,就投井死了。后经众人捞起,全身发蓝,已中毒身亡,大家才知温琼说的是真话。为了纪念这位舍身救人的温琼秀才,百姓就奉他为神。后来,皇帝封他为忠靖王,为东岳泰山神所属的元帅,其全称为"东岳从兵翊灵昭武侯温天君忠靖圣王",所以叫东岳爷;因为他是温州人,老百姓一直称他"温元帅"。其神塑像为蓝面、蓝手、蓝脚,象征中毒身亡。因此,温州民间一直把温元帅看成是驱瘟逐疫之神。

well water was clean and clear, and we drink it everyday. Why are you saying that it is poisonous?" Some people laughed at him, "The scholar becomes bewildered by reading books."

After Wen Qiong cannot persuade others, he stood on the high wellbore and said, "If you don't believe me, I will test the water by myself!" He jumped into the well and was dead. After people scooped him up, his body became blue, he died of poisoning, and people knew that his words were true. In order to commemorate the scholar Wen Qiong who sacrificed his life to save others, common people worshiped him as a god. He was made King Loyalty and Peace by the emperor, he was the marshal under the supervision of the God of Tai Mountain, the eastern peak, and his full name was "Eastern Sacred Mountain Army Supporter, Nobleman of Illustrious Martial Might, Heavenly General Wen, and King of Loyalty and Peace", so he was called "Lord of Eastern Peak"; because he came from Wenzhou, common people called him "Marshal Wen". His image had blue face, blue hands and blue feet, which symbolized the death of poisoning. Therefore, common people of Wenzhou have regarded Marshal Wen as the god dispelling plague.

People held sacrifice ceremony on lunar March 3rd and invited the image of King of Loyalty and Peace to patrol, cloth sheds were set up and lanterns were hung along passages. Huang Han's *The Supplement of Ou* quoted the *Record of Xuehui King Splitting His Soul and Blessing the Temple* that, "This is the convention of Ou at present. There is a ceremony meeting King of Loyalty and Peace every year… The folk convention uses gods in operas." The procedures of inviting gods to patrol started from the selected date, the temple chief used the cup to ask the gods and select the dates, then wrote the patrol notifications in red, and posted them on city gates and streets. On the patrol day, people carried six pairs of flying tiger flags and tablets with the characters such as "Silence and Debarment", "Carrying out Transformation on Behalf of the Heaven", "The Heavenly Gate Isn't Forbidden", "Dispelling Evil Spirits and Diseases", "Blessing and Good Luck", "Loyal and Peaceful Holy King" and so on. The banners, flags and umbrellas followed, and there were five "ghosts" who were acted by five beggars, the rear supervisor was called "Fangxiang" who led one hundred followers to dispel diseases in four seasons, which was nicknamed "Pathbreaker". There were a team of men wearing black hats as high as one *chi* and black clothes on the horses, "Seven Malefics" riding the horses, and "Seven-star Kings" wearing yellow jackets. Four men wearing yellow clothes carried the seal of King of Loyalty and Peace and Incense Burner Pavilion. A golden-faced marshal wearing

到了每年农历三月三，举行祭祀仪式，人们请忠靖王像出巡，通行大道多设布棚，张灯挂彩。黄汉《瓯乘补》引《学惠王灵分佑庙记》说："今瓯俗。每岁上已忠靖王迎会……俚俗以神为戏事。"请神出巡的程序从择日开始，庙董用杯问神选定日期后写出标红（出巡文告），张贴在各个城门和通街大道。出巡当天，先由人扛着飞虎旗和头牌六对，上书"肃静回避""代天行化""天门无禁""驱瘟逐疫""赐福降祥""忠靖圣王"等字样。后面跟着旌旗和伞，然后是雇乞丐扮"五鬼"五人，押队的是"帅百隶而四时逐疫"的"方相氏"，俗称"开路神"。再跟着的是头戴尺余高的青纱帽子、穿着黑衣，骑在马上的一队人，以及骑马的"七煞星"，穿着黄马褂的"七星王"。穿着黄衣的四个人抬着忠靖王印和香炉亭，由身穿金甲的金脸元帅抱着一只令箭，端坐在

明銮，身后跟着许过愿的善男信女装扮成的罪犯们。他们由于身体不好或者遇到过其他不好的事情，被说成是因为前生罪孽未清，这样一装扮的话可以借忠靖王的法力消除罪债。之后才是八人抬着的温元帅銮驾，金光闪耀。东岳神巡行一周需要一二十天，在此期间还有各种娱乐活动，商店也趁机甩卖商品，街头到处都是商贩，还有各种土特产，人们也纷纷走到街上观看各种戏剧。温元帅归殿以后，各里要凑钱搭台演戏，被称为"平安戏"，这时候人们挤到台前，到处人山人海。三月三祭拜温元帅的习俗从宋代开始，盛行于明清，直到民国时期都还非常流行①。

golden armors was seated with an arrow of authority and was judging, and was followed by criminals who were acted by devoted believers who had made wishes. Because they were in bad conditions or met bad things, they were thought that they didn't pay off their sins in their pre-life, and their dressing up in this way can get rid of their sins and debts with the supernatural power of King of Loyalty and Peace. Then eight people carried the imperial carriage of Marshal Wen, which was shining. One circle of the patrol of Eastern Sacred Mountain needed ten to twenty days, there were various kinds of recreational activities in this period, shops took the chance to sell goods at cut-throat prices, there were peddlers and all kinds of local special goods everywhere on streets, and common people went to streets to watch operas. After Marshal Wen returned to the hall, people made a raise to set up platforms to perform operas, which were called "operas of peace". At that time, many people crowded in front of the platform. The convention worshiping Marshal Wen on March 3rd started from the Song Dynasty, flourished in the Ming and Qing Dynasties, and was popular till the period of the Republic of China①.

---

①叶大兵编，《浙江民俗》，甘肃人民出版社，2003年10月第1版，242页

---

①Zhejiang Folk Customs, ed. by Ye Dabing, Oct. 2003, Version 1, p242

"Fair Meeting Sages" is held on March 3rd in other places of Zhejiang, people from all directions come to participate in the parade, and the queue is as long as several *li*, and there are various kinds of colorful flags, gongs and drums and drum operas etc. At last, people carry two statues, one has black face, and the other has red face. Why do local people worship these two divine statues on March 3rd?

It was said that there was a well on the graveyard under Hutou Rock of Danya Mountain in Zhejiang, and the well water was very clear and sweet. This well had a unique character that it was as full as ordinary times when there was a draught and river water became dry. Therefore, common people in nearby villages liked to drink the well water.

浙江其他地方还有在三月初三举办"迎圣会"的习俗，人们从四面八方赶来参加游行，队伍长达数里，还有各种彩旗、锣鼓、花鼓戏等。最后，人们还要抬着两尊像，一个黑面、一个红面。当地人为什么要在三月初三这一天崇敬这两尊神像呢？

据说，很久以前，浙江丹崖山虎头岩下的坟地上有口水井，井水清澈见底，喝在嘴里说不出的甜。这口井还有个奇特处，每逢天旱河水干枯时，井水仍像平时那样满。因此附近村子里的老百姓都吃这口井里的水。

离水井不远的山脚下，搭着一间茅棚。茅棚里住着两个人。舅舅姓周，为人正直善良，品行端正，做事处处行好心，给人行方便，因此大家都叫他周三行。外甥姓章，也跟舅舅一样，是个善良的人，人们就叫他章良。舅甥俩本来不是当地人，是从外地逃荒到洋国，靠种田打柴过日子。

一夜，周三行做了一个奇怪的梦，梦见一个面目

There was a thatched shed near the well under the mountain. Two persons lived in the thatched shed. The family uncle was Zhou, an honest and kindhearted man who was upright in character, did good things and provided convenience to others, and he was named Zhou Sanxing by people. The family name of the nephew was Zhang, he was a good person like his uncle, and was called Zhang Liang by others. They weren't local people, but came from other place to flee from famine, and gathered firewood to make a living.

One night, Zhou Sanxing had a strange dream. He dreamed an ugly Taoist who came to the well and raised his hand to throw a handful of black

sands into the well, and he went forward and scolded the Taoist immediately, "What did you throw into the well? All villagers live on the well, what will people drink since the water became dirty?" The Taoist answered furiously that, "I'm the Plague God, and release plague particularly. I throw plague pills into the well, common people surfer from plague here, and come to see King of Hell!" After hearing his words, Zhou Sanxing was so angry that he rushed towards the Taoist to fight him. The Taoist pushed him with his hand, Zhou Sanxing couldn't stand and his body fell on the well rail… Zhou Sanxing woke from the nightmare, he felt that heartbeat was quickened, so he woke up his nephew. They walked towards the well in the dark. They saw a black shadow moving in the far distance. Zhou Sanxing shouted loudly, and the black shadow disappeared suddenly. Zhou Sanxing suspected and said to Zhang Liang, "Maybe bad people put poison into it, and we bail water to have a try." Zhou Sanxing caught a favorite hen from the roost and forced it to drink the well water. Shortly afterwards, the hen stretched its legs, erected its neck and showed the whites of its eyes, its crest turned black, and it died! They were greatly frightened and hasted to the well quickly.

丑恶的道人来到井边，把手一扬，往井里洒下一把黑色的砂子，他立即上前责问道人："你往井里撒什么?全村的人靠这口井过活，把井水弄脏了，人们怎么吃呢?"那道人恶狠狠地回答说："我是瘟神，专放瘟疫。把瘟丹洒在井里，让这里的百姓都染上瘟疫，去见阎王爷吧!"周三行一听，顿时火冒三丈，冲上前扭住这道人拼命。只见那道人用手一推，周三行站立不住，身子正倒在井栏上……恶梦惊醒，周三行觉得心头直跳，他把外甥叫醒。甥舅两人摸着黑，向井边走去。老远，果然看见一个黑影在移动。周三行大喝一声，那个黑影突然不见了。周三行十分怀疑，章良说："说不定是坏人在放毒，我们舀水来试一试。"周三行从鸡窝里捉出一只心爱的老母鸡，给那只老母鸡灌下去了井水，没多久，那只鸡果然两腿一伸，脖子一挺，眼珠翻白，鸡冠发黑，死了!二人顿时大惊失色，火速赶回到井边。

天亮了，村子里一个名叫正顺的人来挑水。周三行老远喊着："正顺哥，这水不能喝了！"正顺来到井边一愣，说："好好的水，怎么不能吃？"周三行就把母鸡的事全部诉了他。正顺笑了笑说；"老母鸡怕原来就有瘟病的吧？"说着，他提起桶便往井里放。周三行和章良赶紧上前扯住绳子不让打水。挑水的人越来越多了，听了他们舅甥的话，有相信的，也有不相信的，议论纷纷。但大家都知道这舅甥俩平日都是老实人，虽不相信，可也没人敢硬着要打水。

太阳不断升高了，人们没水烧饭，急得全都跑到井边来，黑压压的挤了一大堆。忽然，人群中踱出一个人来，指着周三行的鼻子说："你造谣，到底安什么心？"大家一看，认得他是村子里大财主的儿子金怀中。周三行说："少爷，你说我造谣事小，村里几百条性命的事大。"金怀中三角眼一翻，不住地骂道："你这

Day broke, and a man named Zhengshun in the village came to carry water. Zhou Sanxing shouted from a distance, "Brother Zhengshun, the water cannot be drunk." Zhengshun came to the well and puzzled, "Why can't I drink the water?" Zhou Sanxing told the thing of the dead hen to him. Zhengshun laughed, "Maybe the old hen had the plague originally?" When he said, he put the bucket into the well. Zhou Sanxing and Zhang Liang hasted to hold the rope and didn't let him fetch water. More and more people came to carry water, some people believed their words, some people didn't believe them, and there were many discussions. However, people knew that the uncle and the nephew were honest, and they didn't dare to fetch water.

The sun rose constantly, and they cannot boil rice without water, so they crowded to the well in a hurry. Suddenly, a man came out of the crowd and pointed at the nose of Zhou Sanxing, "What a rumor! What are you up to?" People had a look and recognized him who was Jin Huaizhong, the son of a rich man in the village. Zhou Sanxing said, "Young master, it doesn't matter that you said it's a rumor, but the lives of several hundred of villagers are important." Jin Huaizhong cursed continually that, "Pauper! How is the well water poisonous? Did you put poison into it?" Zhang Liang went forward to explain, Jin Huaizhong shouted furiously, "If anyone doesn't let my long-term laborers carry water, I will tell my father, and send him to the government office to punish him!" Zhou Sanxing found it hard to vindicate himself, and he made his decision, gritted his teeth, crossed the well rail and jumped into the well. It's too late for Zhang Liang to hold him, only a plop was heard, and the well water was splashed as high as several feet. The villagers shouted, "Help! Help!" Jin Huaizhong turned back casually and cursed continuously. Seeing his uncle jumping

穷鬼，好好的井水哪来的毒?要么是你放了毒!"章良上前申辩，金怀小又恶狠狠地吼道："谁不让我家长工挑水，告诉我爹，把他送衙门里去，重重惩办！"周三行见自己有口难分，只得把心一横，牙一咬，跨到井栏边纵身跳了下去，章良连忙拉也来不及只听"扑通"一声，井水溅起了好几尺高。乡亲们立刻大叫起来："快救人，快救人哪?"金怀中却若无其事地往回走，嘴里还骂个不休。章良见舅舅跳了井，吁天抢地地

大哭起来。井边的人群乱了，有的设法下井抢救，有的过来劝慰章良。忽然，井里"突突"地响了起来，如同锅里的水沸腾开了。大家向井里一看，只见黑色的水泡一个接一个不停地往上冒，清冽冽的井水一下子变成黑糊糊的浑泥汤，还透出了一阵阵的恶臭。大家都发了呆。章良拍打着井栏，哭得更加凄惨。井里的黑水"突突突"地冒得更响了，随着大水泡，周三行的头浮上了水面，那脸色乌黑发亮，一双和善的眼睛炯炯发光。几个大胆的村民，一手抓住井拦，一手托起周三行的下颚和后颈，用尽力气把他拉出井面来。章良见了舅舅的尸体，哭得天昏地暗，人日月无光。哭呀，哭呀……泪水哭干了，哭呀，哭呀……眼睛里流出了鲜红的血。血，染红了他整个脸宠。猛听他大叫一声：舅舅啊，舅舅，你死得好惨呀！"章良一口气换不过来，昏倒在周三行旁边，身子顿时僵直了。

into the well, Zhang Liang uttered cries of anguish. People around the well got chaotic, some of them tried to rescue him from the well, and other came to comfort Zhang Liang. Suddenly, the well made a noise like boiling water in pot. People looked at the well, black bubbles rose one by one continuously, and the clear water turned into black mud with foul smell. People stared blankly. Zhang Liang beat the well rail, and cried more sadly. Black water in the well made a louder noise, the head of Zhou Sanxing floated on the surface of the water with large bubbles, his face was black and bright, and the pair of kind eyes beamed. Several bold villagers grasped the well rail with one hand, and supported his lower jaw and back neck and tried their best to pull him out of the well. Zhang Liang saw the black body of his uncle, cried desperately, even the sky became dark and the sun and the moon were dimmed. He cried, even his tears became dry, his eyes bled. The blood reddened his face. Suddenly, he cried, "Uncle, Uncle, you died awfully!" Zhang Liang could't change his breath, he fainted beside Zhou Sanxing, and his body stiffened at once.

It was March 3rd of the Xia Calendar. In order to commemorate the uncle Zhou Sanxing and the nephew, people built a small temple there. They molded statues for them, the uncle had the black face, and the nephew had the red face. There was a horizontal inscribed board on the corridor purlin in the temple, and there were "local guarantee" in four characters. The well was in the middle of the paved path in the temple. The "Fair Meeting Sages" is held on March 3rd every year in order to cherish the memory for the uncle and the nephew who sacrificed themselves to save people.

March 3rd is regarded as an unlucky festival in some places. For example, people in some areas of Hubei Province consider March 3rd the festival for lonely and wild ghosts, which is called "Ghost Festival". Family members prepare rice delicacy on this day, they turn upside down two flat bowls of rice into one bowl in the shape of a dome, place wine and dishes outside to hold sacrifice,they also watch "ghost fire" outdoors in the evening, and practice divination according to conditions of flame motion. They invite opera troupes to perform operas persuading people to do good things, some people go to wild fields to pick up wild vegetables to boil eggs to eat, and it's said that it can make eyes brighter, dispel disasters and avoid misfortunes.

这一天，正是夏历三月初三。为了纪念周三行舅甥两人，人们就在那里建了一座小庙。塑了像，舅舅是黑脸，外甥是红脸。庙殿廊桁上挂着一块匾，上写"一方保障"四个大字。当年的水井就在庙里甬道的正中。每年三月初三的"迎圣"庙会，就是对献身救民的舅甥两人的怀念。

在有些地方，三月初三被认为是不吉祥的一个节日，例如在湖北等地，三月初三被认为是孤魂野鬼的假日，又称之为"鬼节"。在这一天，家里人除了要准备饭馐"将两个平碗饭扣成一碗，呈圆顶形"、酒肴到外举祭以外，晚上还出室看"鬼火"，视火苗移动情况，占卜人事吉凶。还要请戏班子来表演劝人行善的戏本，也有人到野地里掐野菜来煮鸡蛋吃，据说可以亮眼睛，还可以消灾免祸。

位于巴蜀之乡的重庆，每年农历三月初三时，忠县人民都要举行"三月会"。在那一天，不仅有玩龙灯的、舞狮子的，还要抬着土主爷爷的神像上街巡游，锣鼓喧天，热闹无比。村里的农民也走几十里山路到县城里赶上三月会，城里的居民也家家户户张灯结彩，放烟花爆竹，相当热闹。关于这个节日，还有一个很感人的故事。

传说春秋战国时候，忠县城曾经是巴国的一个重要城邑。驻守这个山城的将军叫巴曼子，他是一个贤明的地方官，十分爱护老百姓，人们过着和平安宁的生活。

不幸，有一次巴国突然遭到南面一个邻国的入侵，形势十分危急。巴国国小，又没有防备，一下打了败仗。巴国不得不向东边强大的邻国楚国请求援救。楚国是五霸之一，兵强马壮，他答应了巴国的请求，出兵援救。楚国

Zhongxian County is located in Chongqing, the town of Bashu, people hold "March Fair" on the lunar March 3rd every year, some of them play dragon lanterns, perform lion dance, and carry the divine statue of the Land God in streets to patrol, and there are lively and extraordinary gongs and drums. Farmers of villages walk tens of *li* to the county and take part in March Fair, households in the town hang up lanterns and set off fireworks and crackers, and the scene is animated. As for the festival, there is an impressive story.

It was said that Zhongxian County was once an important city in the period of Spring and Autumn and the Warring States, the general guarding the mountain town was named Ba Manzi, he was a wise local official, took good care of common people very much, and people lived a peaceful and tranquil life.

Unfortunately, the State of Ba was invaded by a neighboring country in the south suddenly, and the condition was rather critical. The State of Ba was small, it didn't take precautions and it lost the battle. The State of Ba had to ask for rescue from the neighboring State of Chu which was powerful in the east. It was one of the five countries, which had strong soldiers and horses, and it granted the request of the State of Ba and dispatched troops to rescue it.

After the State of Chu dispatched troops, enemies of the State of Ba were driven away. However, Prince of Chu was very selfish and greedy, and he had never helped others without extortion, he made a claim and asked the State of Ba to cede three cities to him as compensation. Zhongxian County was one of the cities which Prince of Chu requested to be ceded.

Certainly, Manzi knew that the State of Chu wanted to seek hegemony, and it fought everywhere and flaunted its prowess. Unexpectedly, he had never thought that Prince of Chu would make such a harsh claim. People of the State of Ba were forced to fight, their fields grew wild, their family ruined, and they lived in deep distress, and he cannot bear to let their people come to the State of Chu to have a hard time. People came to meet Manzi, they wanted to repay the State of Chu with other property rather than paying allegiance to the State of Chu.

King of Ba heard people's suggestion and assigned an envoy to see Prince of Chu, "Ba is a small state, it has a few cities, and is willing to offer other property to Prince of Chu, and we want to keep the three cities." The face of Prince of Chu firmed and said, "I will not change my words. You return to transmit my words to King of Ba, he shall

出兵后，巴国的敌人被赶走了。

但楚王是一个十分贪婪的人，他从不白帮忙，刚替巴国赶走了敌人，他便提出一项要求，要巴国割让给他三个城池作报偿。忠县是楚王要求割去的三个城池之一。

曼子固然知道，楚国一心想称霸，东征西伐，耀武扬威。但万万没有料到楚王会提出如此苛刻的条件。巴国人民被迫打仗，田地荒芜，家破人亡，生活在水深火热之中，怎忍心让自己的人民再去楚国受罪?城里的百姓也纷纷来向曼子请求，宁愿以其他财物报偿楚国，决不愿归顾楚国。

巴国国王听了人们的请求，就派使臣去求见楚王说："巴国国小城少，愿意以其他财物奉献楚王，保留三个城池。"楚王却把脸一沉，说："我说出的话，没有改变的。你回去转告巴国国王，快献三个城来，要是再迟延，我将派兵前去讨伐。"

巴国使臣回国，三个城池的百姓听到楚王的无理要求后，人人都满腔义愤，立誓保卫三个城池。曼子更是茶饭不进，坐卧不安。他想：如果割城，百姓不愿。如不割城，楚王以兵相侵，老百姓要遭受更大灾难。他寻思不出对付的办法。

这天，楚国派兵来讨城了，曼子从容不迫地接见了楚国使臣。当使臣逼曼子立字交城的时候，曼子回答说："城里的百姓都不愿去楚国，因此城不能给。我宁愿把我的头颅割下顶替城池作报偿。请使臣带我的头颅去献给楚王。"况完，就取下自己随身佩带的青铜柳叶剑割下了自己的头。

楚国使臣吓得目瞪口呆，只好提着曼子的头颅去报楚王。楚王也吓呆了，他叹息说："既然巴

offer the three cities quickly, and I will send armed forces to suppress him if he delays any more."

The envoy of the State of Ba came back, common people of the three cities became angry after hearing the unreasonable demand of Prince of Chu, and they swore to protect the three cities. Manzi didn't want to eat and was unable to sit down or sleep at ease. He thought that people would not let the cities be ceded. If he didn't cede the cities, Prince of Chu would invade his state with forced armies, and common people would suffer from the greater disaster. He couldn't find a solution.

One day, the State of Chu came to ask for the cities with armies, Manzi received the envoy of the State of Chu calmly. When the envoy forced Manzi to write a covenant to turn over the cities, Manzi answered, "People in the cities don't want to come to the State of Chu, so the cities shall not be ceded. I would rather cut down my head to repay the cities. Please offer my head to Prince of Chu!" After saying his words, he took out his bronze willow leaf sword and cut down his head.

The envoy of the State of Chu was paralyzed with terror, and he had to carry the head of Manzi to report to Prince of Chu. Prince of Chu was terrified and sighed, "Since Ba Manzi doesn't fear death, common people also don't fear death. If common people in the three cities pledge their lives to fight, it's useless to send armies to attack the cities. I have to give up them." In this way, the State of Chu didn't assign armies to attack the cities any more.

Manzi used his head to protect the cites of the State of Ba, and protected peaceful and happy life of common people. People showed their gratitude to him, set up a temple for him, and called it Tuzhu Temple. He cut down his head on March 3rd. People carry his statue to patrol on this day and commemorate him grandly. This day is called "March Fair". It has been passed down for hundreds of years from generation to generation.

Objects worshiped by Cantonese are similar to those of Henan, who are Taoist immortals. On March 3rd, Cantonese go to Northern Emperor Temple to worship. Northern Emperor was also called Xuantian Super Emperor, it was said March 3rd was his birthday. People go to Northern Emperor Temple to burn incense and kowtow, which is very popular. In some places, March 3rd is thought as the birthday of Heavenly Goddess. People hold temple fair to celebrate for Heavenly Goddess for three days and three nights consecutively. Heavenly Goddess was also called Heavenly Empress, her temple was located in Southern Heavenly Harem of Hua City of Wuhua County, and it was built in the late Qing

曼子都这么不怕死，老百姓更不怕死了，如果三城百姓誓死不从，兴兵讨城也没有用，就放弃三城罢了。"这样，楚国再没有派兵讨城了。

曼子用自己的头颅保住了巴国城邑，保住了百姓和平安乐的生活，人们十分感激他，给他立了一个庙，叫土主庙，三月三日，是他砍头的日子。百姓都抬着他的塑像游行，隆重纪念他。这一天，称作"三月会"，千百年来，代代相传。

客家人的三月三所祭拜的对象和河南差不多，都是道教神仙。在三月三的时候，客家地区的人们修建了北帝庙宇来祭拜。北帝又叫玄天上帝，据说三月初三是他的诞辰，人们在这一天去北帝庙宇给他烧香磕头，北帝庙宇的香火非常旺盛。在有些地区，三月初三被认为是天妃娘娘的生日，届时要举办庙会为天妃娘娘庆贺，一连举办三天三夜。天妃

娘娘又名天后，天妃庙址在五华县华城之南天后宫，始建于清末民初时期，县城以及附近的百姓都非常信奉天妃，所以三月三的庙会也是当地的一大盛会了。

天妃庙前有一块长方形的空地，另一端是一个固定的戏台，被称为"天妃戏棚"，庙会期间，人们就在空地上观看庙会戏台演出。整个庙会从起会开始分为三个阶段：起会——出巡——回迎，但每一个程序都有繁琐的、固定的规矩。

Dynasty and the early Republic of China. However, common people in the county and nearby believe in Heavenly Goddess, and the March 3rd temple fair is one of local grand ceremonies.

There is a rectangular opening in front of Heavenly Goddess Temple, and there is a fixed stage on the other end, which is called "Heavenly Goddess Stage", the masses come to the opening to appreciate stage performance during temple fair. The whole temple fair is divided into three stages, i.e. starting ceremony, patrol and meeting, but each procedure has complicated and fixed stipulations.

Starting: Ceremony starts from March 22nd, the prime ministers and chiefs holding the temple fair assemble in Heavenly Goddess Temple and begin to hold temple fair. They urge businessmen and people to participate in decorating the Colorful Flower Street, and launch devout men and women to organize the gong and drum group, and the artistic group follows the Goddess to patrol on March 23rd. As for the Colorful Flower Street, the cloth curtains are used to shield the streets overhead, various kinds of paper flowers and colorful lanterns are hung under the cloth curtains, and the streets are decorated beautifully; the colorful lanterns are lighted in the evening, and the streets become crystal palaces of light and color.

Since the starting, red lanterns are hung up before Heavenly Goddess Temple, red couplets are stuck, there are brilliant candle light and fragrant incense in the temple; "Flute Shed" is set up on the outdoor opening; buglers play as scheduled; opera troupes in Heavenly Goddess Temple begin to perform operas on schedule (most players are from "Linhua Hall", which is Puppet Line Opera Troupe of Wuhua County), day operas start from two o'clock to five o'clock on the afternoon of March 22nd; early night operas begin at eight o'clock in the evening. The day and early night operas are called "formal plays", including traditional opera acts such as Three Tricks on Zhou Yu, Drowning Jinshan Mountain and the Tang Priest's Journey for

起会：所谓起会，即从：三月廿二开始，凡主持本届庙会的总理、首事集中于天妃庙开始正式执事主持庙会。其中主要的是发动商民"彩花街"和发动善男信女组织锣鼓队伍，文艺队伍于三月二十三跟随"天妃娘娘出巡"。"彩花街"就是用布幕把街道上空遮蔽，然后在布幕下挂上各种纸花、彩灯，把街道装饰得花团锦簇。晚上把彩灯点亮，街道顿时变成五彩缤纷如晶宫。

从起会开始，天妃庙前红灯高桂，红联张贴，庙内烛光辉照，香烟缭绕；门外空地上搭起的"笛棚"，吹鼓手如期吹打；"天妃戏棚的戏班（多数雇请五华县木偶线剧团"林华堂"）按期开锣演戏，一般是三月二十二下午2点左右开始"做日戏"到5点左右为止；夜晚8点左右·做上夜戏"，这种日戏和上夜戏皆演传统的《水浒》《三国》《西游记》《白蛇传》中的诸如《三戏周瑜》《水淹金山》《唐僧取经》等戏本，称之为"正本戏"。午夜之后至天亮之前，则演调笑一类的小品，称之为"下夜耍戏"。有一个不成文的规矩，日戏和上夜戏的"正本"，男女老幼皆看。"下夜戏"为妇女、小孩所不宜，只是成年男子观看。约定俗成的是，庙会期间，妇女和小孩看戏到晚上12点之前。因此，午夜之后便是男人的世界。

上表：所谓上表，就是组织善男信女在庙会期间专门参拜天妃，并在参拜后在天妃神坛前抽签产生下届的庙会主持者——首事，并称之为"拈首事"。如果抽出的"红签"纸上写有"首事"字样，那么这个上表人即"当选"为下届庙会的"首事"。上表仪式结束后，上表人可择时在庙会即席就餐一次，叫"坐流水席"。

Scriptures etc. from *Outlaws of the Marsh, Three Kingdoms, Journey to the West* and *the Story of the White Snake*. From midnight to dawn, some short funny acts are performed, which are called "late funny night plays". There is an informal stipulation that men and women can watch "formal plays" of daily and early night operas; women and children are improper to watch "late night plays", and only men can watch them. According to the long established practice, women and children watch operas before twelve o'clock at midnight, and they will leave automatically, so it's the world of men after midnight.

Listing: As for listing, devout men and women worship Heavenly Goddess during temple fair especially, and the president of the next temple fair will be made through drawing lots in front of the divine platform of Heavenly Goddess Temple after worshiping. This event is called "picking up the chief". If the characters of "the chief" are written on the red lot, the listing person is "elected" as the "chief" of the next temple fair. After the completion of the listing ceremony, the listing people can dine in the temple fair on chosen time, which is called "having open banquet".

Patrol: This is the most important and solemn ceremony of the temple fair, people carry the divine statue and table of Heavenly Goddess to patrol in the streets, which is very grand.

The attending teams are mainly composed of devout men when meeting, all of them wear the formal attire, which is the gown named "Sayi", wear hat and glasses, hold long and circular red lanterns written with names and hall titles, and some of them ride horses or sit in sedans to show their identities. The folk gong and drum and making-up teams of different clan organizations join in the procession especially, which show dignity and force of the patrol ceremony, the gong and drum teams are divided into large gong and drum class and small gong and drum class; the large gong and drum class is composed of a dozen of people at least and tens of people at most, they play dozens of percussion instruments such as large drums, high gongs and large cymbals etc., which are accompanied with conches and *suona*. Most making-up performances are organized by street businessmen and common people, especially Northern Gate Street and Heavenly Goddess Street. As for the making-up performances, young boys and girls dress up as ancient or fairy characters such as "boy and girl attendants of fairies", "celestial beauty scattering flowers" and "a fairy old man flying on a crane", they are fixed on the sedans with all kinds of shapes and instruments and are carried by people, which is called "acting stories". Folk gong and drum

出巡：即抬着天妃神像神位牌往各条街道出行，这是庙会最重要最庄严的仪式，十分隆重。

出迎时的簇拥队伍多为善男，他们不论老少皆穿礼服，俗称"洒衣"的长衫，他们要戴礼帽、眼镜，手特长圆形写明姓氏堂号的红灯笼，有的还骑马，坐轿以示身份。特别是队伍中掺进各街道、姓氏或宗族组织的民间锣鼓队伍和化妆队伍，大大显示出巡仪式的庄严、威武，锣鼓队伍分大锣鼓班和小锣鼓班。大锣鼓班少则十几人，多则几十人组成，敲打大鼓、高锣、大钹等几十件打击乐器，并伴海螺、唢呐吹奏。至于化妆表演，多为街道商民所组织，尤以南门街，天后街为最。化妆表演的形式，多以少男少女化妆成"金童玉女"、"天女散花"，"仙翁乘鹤"等古装或神话人物，用各种造型器具固定于轿架上，然后由人抬着游行，俗称

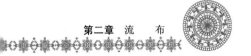
"扮故事"。民间锣鼓班和"扮故事"均为年年"三月三",是最为百姓喜闻乐见的形式,给群众增添了极大乐趣。

在庙会期间,戏班子除了表演戏本之外,还有各种精彩表演,而商铺也趁这个热闹时候招徕客人,前来观看的老百姓都是一个挤一个,别提多有气氛了,都说"三月三,换白衫,有钱冇(无)钱街上尖(蹅)。"

teams and "acting stories" are held on March 3rd yearly, and they are the forms which common people are pleased to hear and see and add great pleasure to common people.

During the temple fair, the opera troupe performs opera texts, and provides various kinds of wonderful performances, shops attract guests on this rumbling occasion, common people crowd together to watch, the atmosphere is so lively, and there is the saying that "people change white shirts on March 3rd, rich and poor people crowd on streets."

3 多彩民族
Colorful Minorities

In the long history, there are various kinds of cultural communications and disseminations among national minorities. Many minorities celebrate March 3rd, but they have different folklores and origins related to it. Take Hezhe people as an example, they come to sacrifice to mountain and rvier gods. Shaman witches play sacrifice dances to worship gods on March 3rd and September 9th, which is related to the natural environment of Hezhe people.

历史长河里，各个民族之间一直有各种文化交流和传播，很多的民族在三月初三这一天也纷纷庆贺，只不过与之相关的民间传说和起源不一样而已。就拿赫哲族来说，赫哲族每逢三月三和九月九，就要去祭祀山神、河神，萨满巫师还要跳祭祀舞蹈敬神仙。这和赫哲族所生活的自然环境有关。

很久很久以前，在松花江和黑龙江汇合的三江口南岸，申哈里狩猎部族有户打猎人家。有一年，打春刚过，眼瞧着山坡漫岗，河三叉沟边的积雪快要融化了。猎人扛起扎枪，背上装满粮食、肉干的皮囊，辞别了自己的妻子，朝着猎犬，踏着冰封的江面，到遥远的黑龙江北岸山里去打貂皮。

猎人走后，闪下妻子孤零零一个人在家。有一天晚上，媳妇刚要躺下睡觉，就听门外有扑通、扑通的声音直响，她吓得赶忙摸火镰，打火石。点着灯一看，只见门外伸进一只老虎爪子，脚掌上扎了一根苕条根刺儿，血一个劲地往下淌。媳妇寻思，这老虎是让我帮它拔掉脚掌上扎的刺吧。于是，回身从桦皮篓子里找出一只镊子，夹住刺儿往外拔。可惜镊子夹不住，刺儿也没拔出来。怎么办？媳妇只好用双手扳着老虎爪子，用自己的牙齿咬着刺儿，狠劲地拔了出来。然

It was said that Shenhali hunting clan had a hunter household in Sanjiangkou Sorthern Bank at the junction of Songhua River and Heilongjiang River. One year, snow piled on slopes, rolling hills and ditches beside rivers was to melt soon in the early spring. The hunter carried his gun on his shoulder, carried the leather bags with grains and dried meat on his back, departed from his wife, crossed the frozen river surface with his hound to hunt for fur of martens in the mountain in the Northern Bank of Heilongjiang River.

After the hunter left, his wife stayed at home lonely. When his wife was going to lie down and sleep one evening, she heard that there were plops outside the door, she was so scared that she made a fire with a flint. She saw a claw of a tiger outside the door with the light, and there was a sweet potato thorn in its paw, which bled continuously. His wife thought that this tiger wanted her to pull out the thorn. Then she turned back and found a pair of tweezers from a leather bag, nipped the thorn and tried to pull it out. It was such a pity that the tweezers couldn't nip the thorn. How to deal with it? The wife used his hands to push its claw, and bit the thorn with her teeth, and pulled it out forcefully.

Afterwards, she cleaned the blood on its claw with water, put a little salt and flour on it and let it leave.

Afterwards, the tiger came to the door of the wife every two or three days and threw a roe, deer, wild boar or goat. After the hunter came back, he knew it and brought some foods to send them to the tiger in order to thank it for taking care of his wife. He looked for the tiger in all directions, but he couldn't find it, then he put the foods in the mountain, sacrificed a cup of wine towards the forest, and went for hunting. He hunted a lot of animals successfully on that day, and he felt surprised and told it after returning home. Afterwards, hunters sacrificed to the tiger as sacrificing to the Mountain God, saw March 3rd and September 9th as the festivals in the hunting harvest seasons in spring and autumn and held grand sacrifice activities. On the occasion, Shamans wore the divine shirts with the bronze mirror and the waist bells, wore the three, four, five, six, seven or eight-forked divine hats, held the divine sticks with snake skin, struck the divine drums, sang songs and played the happy deer god dance with the beats. They celebrated lucky hunting, and wished Shenhali hunting clan had a flourishing population each year.

后，又用水把老虎脚掌子上的血迹擦洗干净，上了点盐面，就把老虎打发走了。

从此以后，老虎三天两头来到媳妇家门口，不是扔只狍子和鹿，就是扔头野猪和山羊。猎人回来后，知道了这件事，为了感谢老虎对自己妻子的照顾，带了一些食品进山去送给它吃。可是东找西寻，找不到那老虎，便将食品放在山上，对着山林敬了一杯酒，自己就打围去了。那天他顺利地打到了许多猎物，心里暗暗称奇。回家后就把这事告诉了大家。以后进山打用的猎人，就把老虎当作山神爷老把头，每逢春秋两季狩猎丰收时节——三月三和九月九就要举行隆重的祭祀活动。那一天，萨满们穿上佩有青铜镜的神裙，挎上腰铃，穿上三叉、四叉、五叉、六叉、七叉或八叉的神帽，挂着套有蛇皮的神杖，敲着神鼓，踏着咚咚的节拍，载歌载舞，跳起了欢快的鹿神舞。大家欢庆出猎如意，祝愿申哈里狩猎部族年年岁岁人丁兴旺。

这个风习，直到新中国成立前夕还有。就是到了今天，在丰收的网滩上，在林中的篝火旁，在逢年过节欢宴的时候，每当举起酒杯时，猎民的子孙们都要用手指沾几滴美酒，撮撮地弹向空中，表示赫哲人对老虎的敬意。

赫哲族世代居住在山林里，这种对大自然的崇敬之情，也是长期以来人类与自然和谐共处的结果。在彩云之南，鹤庆的白族、彝族、汉族、丽江的纳西族，还有中甸、德钦的藏族，人们都要穿红着绿，大家唱着各族山歌、小调，去朝鹤庆石宝山。根据当地的民间传说，人们去朝山，一是拜谒开辟鹤庆坝子的年伽佗祖师，二是去呼唤张氏兄妹回乡。张氏兄妹是何许人也？他们是为了当地人们幸福而牺牲的善良人儿。

The convention lasted till the founding of People's Republic of China. The later generations of the hunter spray several drops of delicious wine with their fingers and throw them into the sky to show Hezhe people's respect to tigers when they raise goblets on the net beach, beside the bonfire in the forest on the occasions of festivals and feasts.

Hezhe people have lived in the mountain forests for generations, and their worship towards nature has been the harmonious result between human beings and nature. In the south of the colorful cloud, Bai people, Yi people, Han people of Heqing, Naxi people of Lijiang, Tibetans of Zhongdian and Deqin wear red and green clothes, they sing mountain songs and popular tunes of minorities, and make a pilgrimage to Shifou Mountain of Heqing. According to the local folklore, people make a pilgrimage to the mountain to worship the master Mou Gatuo who created Heqing Plain and call Zhang siblings to return the village. Who were Zhang siblings? They were good people who sacrificed their life for happiness of local people.

Mou Gatou hooked and dispelled the tadpole dragon, turned the sea into fields, then Bai people on the four mountains of Heqing moved to settle in the plain consecutively. However, there were no the sun or crops such as paddy rice, wheat and broad bean etc. People brought some seeds of sweet buckwheat and oats, but they couldn't live in the plain. Therefore, people conquered the tadpole dragon and didn't suffer from the misfortune of the furious dragon, but the days were hard without the sun and grains.

There was a household whose family name was Zhang, the father and the mother were honest and tolerant weavers, fostered three sons and a daughter, and they were filial and obedient children. The name of the oldest brother was Zhang Qin who was eighteen years old, the name of the second brother was Zhang Zhi who was fifteen years old, the name of the third sister was Zhang Xian, who was thirteen years old, the youngest brother was Zhang Ci, who was ten years old. The family thought over finding the sun to help growth of grains at times. Especially, Zhang siblings consulted the old men on where they can find the sun and the grains at their leisure.

年伽佗钓走蝌蚪龙，把大海变为桑田后，鹤庆四山头上的白族人民，都陆续搬到坝子里来安居。可是，这地方没有太阳，也没有稻谷、小麦、蚕豆等农作物。人们从山头上带来了些甜荞燕麦种，但在坝子里总是种不活。所以，人们虽治服了蝌蚪龙，不再遭受凶龙的祸害，可是，没有太阳和粮食，日子还是难熬。

张家村有一户人家，爹妈是忠厚本分的织布匠，养了三个儿子和一个姑娘，都是孝心好、肯听话的好儿女。十八岁的大哥叫张勤，十五岁的二哥叫张智，三姑娘叫张贤，刚满十三岁，幺兄弟才十岁，叫张慈。他们一家人，时时为寻找太阳利粮食而盘算着。尤其是张氏兄妹，一有空，就去向老年人请教——到底到哪里能找到太阳和粮食？

一天，张氏四兄妹从百岁老人那里打听到太阳的住处和粮食的长处。他们经过商量，决定去寻找太阳和粮食。他们回到家里，向父母讲述了自己的打算。阿爹又高兴，又难过；阿妈又喜欢，又伤心。阿爹对儿女说："你们兄妹四人有这个决心，让我喜欢。人生在世，能为大家多做好事就是做人的根本。不过，此一去，山高水深，路途遥远，望你们兄妹要齐心协力，互助互爱。勤儿，你要多多关照弟妹们。你们三个小的，要听哥哥的话。不管遇到什么困难，只要想到一百零八村的乡亲在等着你们，就有了战胜困难的力量了。"阿妈对儿女说："我能生养你们这样的儿女，也不枉来人世一转。出远门不比在家，你们在路上要眼观四路，耳听八方，天不黑就投宿，雀出林才起身。"

四兄妹看着两鬓如雪的爹娘，心中十分难过。他们不忍心丢下两位老

One day, Zhang siblings knew the places of the sun and the grains from a centenarian. They decided to look for them after the negotiation. They returned home, and they told about their plan to their parents. The father was pleased as well as feeling sorry; the mother was happy and sad. The father said to his children, "I am glad to see your decision. It's fundamental for people to do good things for others in their life. However, your far journey is full of high mountains and deep rivers, and I hope that your siblings shall make concerted efforts, respect and love each other. Qin, you must take care of your siblings. You three young children shall listen to the words of your brother. No mater what difficulties you meet, you will have the force to conquer them if you think that the villagers of one hundred and eight villages are waiting for you." The mother told their children, "I'm proud of having the children like you. You must be observant and alert on the way, because traveling isn't like being at home, you shall seek temporary lodging before it is dark, and set off after the sun rises."

The four siblings looked at their old parents who already had grey hair, and felt sorry. They cannot bear to leave the two old people, and asked the youngest brother to serve their parents at home. One day, the oldest brother carried oat flour milled by the mother, the second brother carried two gourds of water of hometown, and the third sister carried the long knife of the father, left their parents, departed from the villagers seeing them off, and walked towards the eastern Shifou Mountain.

Before leaving, Zhang Qin persuaded his brother Zhang Ci, "My youngest brother, you must take care of our parents, and comfort them. When you see the sun rising from Shifou Mountain, we will come back. We will find the sun and the grains and come back to reunite with you before Tomb-Sweeping Day of the next year."

The siblings left their parents and villagers, and they spent ninety-nine days on ninety-nine rivers and mountains and arrived in the Drilling Sky Slope, which had sheer cliffs, and the tip hid in the clouds and the fog. There wasn't a road, even not a place upon which feet could stand. The third sister cannot walk any more, the second brother cannot climb any more, Zhang Qin was tired and felt sluggish. In order to look for the sun and the grains, Zhang Qin was quite unconscious of fatigue, he carried

人，便叫幺弟在家服侍爹娘。一天，大哥背着阿妈磨的燕麦炒面，老二挂着两葫芦家乡水，三妹背着阿爹的长刀，离开了爹妈，辞别了送行的乡亲，朝东面的石缶山方向走去。

临行时，张勤劝弟弟张慈说："幺弟，在家中要好好孝顺爹妈，多用宽心话安慰老人。当你看到石确山顶冒出太阳时，我们就回来了。明年清明节前，我们就会找到太阳和粮食回家团聚的。"

张勤兄妹离开了爹妈和乡亲，走了九十九天，过了九十九大河，爬了九十九座大山，来到了钻天坡。这钻天坡悬崖峭壁，山尖躲在云雾中。莫说是路，连站脚的地方也没有。三妹走不动了，二弟爬不起来了，张勤也累得浑身无力。但为了寻找太阳和粮食，张勤顾不上劳累，背起三妹，牵着二弟，一步一步向山顶爬去。

兄妹三人爬上山顶，已累行爬不动了，只能坐下喘口气，谁知，山上狂风怒吼，飞沙走石，连人都快要被刮走。兄妹三人，互相搀扶，跌跌撞撞，找到了一个避风的崖洞。进到洞里，只见一个白发苍苍，面黄肌瘦，骨瘦如柴的老妈妈躺在地上呻吟。三兄妹上前问道："老奶奶，您怎么了，为什么一个人躺在这里？"老妈妈翻了翻眼睛，有气无力地说道："我是五谷神婆，专管人间的五谷神种。五百年前，我要到玉龙雪山上去传播五谷。走到这里，被风魔大王拦劫，抢去了五谷神种。我拼命争夺，只抢回了三颗。谁知，它在山上布满了风兵风将，使我无法逃脱远走。我怕神种搁久了，不会萌发，便在这山洞旦把神种种下了。尤其怕风魔再来抢夺这剩下的三颗神种，五百年来，我寸

the third sister, led the second brother, and climbed towards the top step by step.

The three siblings climbed to the top, were too tired to climb any more, and sat to have a rest. Unexpectedly, the wind howled furiously, the sand and wind was flying, and even people would be blown away. They supported with each other, staggered and found a cliff cave to shelter from the wind. When they entered the cave, a pale and thin old woman lay on the ground and groaned. The three siblings came up and asked, "Old grandmother, what's wrong? Why do you lie there?" The old woman gazed and said weakly, "I'm the Divine Mother of the Five Cereals, and manage the seeds of the five cereals on the earth. Five hundred years ago, I came to Yulong Snow Mountain to sow the five cereals. When I came here, I was intercepted and the seeds of the five cereals were robbed by King of Wind Monster. I risked my life to fight him, and only got three grains. He had many wind soldiers and generals on the mountain, and I couldn't escape. I feared that the divine seeds couldn't germinate if they were held too long, and I sowed them in this cave. I fear that the Wind Monster will come to rob the rest three divine seeds, so I haven't left the cave for five hundred years. I haven't eaten or drunk and become weak." After saying the words, she closed her eyes.

The three siblings took out fried flour and water which they carried in a hurry, made it into porridge and fed it to the old mother. The food completely restored the old woman, and she was willing to talk. After inquiring them and knowing their experience, the old woman said happily, "Well, you come to look for the grains, and you find the right person. I send these three divine seeds to you and complete one of my wishes." The three siblings jumped happily, "Old mother, you are so kind." The old woman asked them to help her up. They saw three golden seeds on the place which she lay on, including amber paddy rice, golden wheat and silver broad bean.

The old woman told the siblings, "These three seeds will come out, grow up and bear fruits after ninety-nine days. They can be reaped and taken away after they bear fruits. The seeds which are born within ninety-nine days cannot live anywhere." After saying the words, the old woman turned into a rosy cloud and flied away.

步不离洞。没吃没喝，身体渐渐消瘦了。"说完，神婆又闭上了眼睛。

兄妹三人，赶忙拿出随身带来的炒面和水，调成汤糊，给老妈妈喂下。老妈妈吃了东西，有了精神，话也多起来了。询问后，得知三兄妹的来历，老妈妈高兴地说："好了，你们既是为人们去寻找粮食，现刻可算找到主了。我就把这三颗神种送给你们，也了却我的一桩心愿。"三兄妹喜欢得跳了起来："老奶奶，您真好。"老妈妈叫三兄妹把她扶起来。就在她躺卧的地方，他们看见了三颗金光灿烂的种子——琥珀般的稻谷，黄金样的小麦，白银似的蚕豆。

老妈妈告诉张勤兄妹："再等九十九天，这三颗种子才能出苗长大结出果实。到结了果实，才能收割带走。不到九十九天结出的种子，不管带到那里去，都种不活。"老妈妈说完，化作一道彩霞飘走了。

三兄妹经过商量，决定让三妹留在洞中守卫神种苗。两个哥哥依依不舍地离开了石洞。

张勤、张智弟兄，离开了石洞。又走了九十九天，爬了九十九座大山，杀死了九十九只老熊，劈死了九十九条蟒蛇，到达了南天门。这南天门是银龙的老窝，终年冰雪不化，随时都飞雹洒雪，连石头都冰冻了。弟兄二人还未走近南天门，银龙便喷出蛋大的冰雹，劈头盖脸打来，打得兄弟二人浑身青肿。张勤看弟弟被打得鲜血满身，扑上前去，用自己的身体护住弟弟。张智在哥哥的身下看得真切：南天门下有一个口朝天的石洞，银龙从那石洞中出进。冰雹、飞雪也随银龙的出进而急缓。张智看见银龙一进洞，便把哥哥一掀，挣起身来，几步奔向石洞，一屁股坐在上边，把个石洞盖的严丝合缝。顷刻，满天冰雹、雪花便止住了。张勤忙去拉弟弟时，弟弟已被冰冻在石洞口上了。张勤流着眼泪，拉死拉活，怎么也

After negotiation, the three siblings decided that the third sister stayed in the cave to guard the divine seedlings. The two brothers left the cave reluctantly.

After the two brothers left the cave, they walked ninety-nine days, climbed ninety-nine mountains, killed ninety-nine old bears, split ninety-nine boas to death, and arrived at the Northern Heaven Gate, which was the hideout of the silver dragon. The ice and snow didn't melt, the hail and snow always flew, and even the stones were frozen. Before the two brothers approached the Southern Heaven Gate, the silver dragon blew out egg-sized hail on the two brothers, and their bodies became black and blue. Zhang Qin saw his brother bleeding on the whole body, threw himself forward, and used his body to protect his younger brother. Zhang Zhi looked clearly under the body of his brother, there was a cave with an upturned entrance, and the silver dragon came in and out from the cave. Hail stones and flying snow became fast or slow when the silver dragon came in or out of it. When Zhang Zhi saw the silver dragon coming into the cave, he turned over his brother, stood up and ran to the cave in steps, sat on it and covered the cold cave entrance completely. Zhang Qin cried,and tried his best to pull his brother, but he couldn't move him. Zhang Zhi floundered and said to Zhang Qin brokenly, "Brother, please don't be sorry. If you pull me out from the cave, the silver dragon will fly out and throw snow and hail. Both of us will freeze to death.

Who will go to look for the sun? The Southern Heaven Gate is the only passage to the east, and many people will come here hereafter, and go to the east to look for happiness. I vanquish the silver dragon, and pave the road for coming and going of people. Although I die here, I am pleased. Our father often told us 'one shall do good things for others'. Do it in this way, our parents will be glad if they know it. However, we are brothers, and we will not play and chop wood together any more. Afterwards, the burden of taking care of our parents shall be carried by you." After saying the words, he died at the cave entrance under the Southern Heaven Gate with smile.

Zhang Qin overcame his grief, cleaned the blood stains on the body of his brother, and took off one of his sheep skin coat, buried the body of his brother with snow, carried the long knife and climbed towards the east. Zhang Qin overcame his grief and pain, climbed the mountains for ninety-nine day and arrived at the Great Black Mountain. A furious tiger which had the size of ninety-nine elephants lived in the Great Black Cave. The sun shining the world

拉不动弟弟。张智挣扎着，断断续续地对张勤说："哥哥，别难过。假使现在你把我从洞口上救下来，银龙就会飞出降雪洒雹。我们两人同时都会冻死在这里，那谁又去寻找太阳呢?再说，这南天门又是通往东方的一条独路，今后还有多少人要从这里走过，去东方寻找幸福。我既降伏了银龙，又为来往的人铺平了道路，虽死在这里，也很高兴。阿爸常教我们：'人活在世，就是要为大家多做好事'。今天我这样做了，爹妈知道，也会喜欢的。不过，我们弟兄，再不能一齐玩耍，一齐砍柴了。从今以后，孝敬爹妈的重担，就落在你和弟妹身了。"张智说完，含笑死在南天门下的银龙洞口。

张勤忍住悲痛，用雪抹去了弟弟的满身血痕，脱下了自己穿着的一件羊皮褂给弟弟披上，再用雪把弟弟的尸体埋好，才背上长刀，一直向东方爬去。张勤含悲忍痛，又爬了九十九天的大山，最后，来到了大黑山中。大黑山的大黑洞中，住着一只有九十九头象大的猛虎。普照天地的太阳，就是被这只猛虎吞到肚子里去了。猛虎被灼热的太阳把肚子烧得受不住的时候，它便把太阳吐出来玩。这时，天地间才有一线光亮。待猛虎把太阳玩厌了，又吞回肚里去，天地便一片漆黑。

张勤到了大黑洞口，正见猛虎把太阳当作一个火球在玩耍。他顾不得浑身疲劳，举着长刀，向猛虎冲去。猛虎急忙把太阳吞到肚里，用尾巴一扫，就把张勤扫到了半空中。幸好张勤抓住一朵白云，他躺在白云上想法治服猛虎。想来想去，决定钻进老虎肚里去取太阳。

白云渐渐往下落，在一棵松树尖上，张勤抓住树枝，慢慢爬下树来。他走了九天九夜，又来到大黑洞口。猛虎见来了人，张开大口，就要吞食张勤。张勤忙用长刀，忍痛割下腿上的一块肉丢给猛

was swallowed into the stomach of this furious tiger. The violent tiger cannot bear the scorching sun and spit it out to play with it. At this moment, there was a light in the world. When the tiger was bored with the sun, it swallowed the sun again, and the world became dark.

When Zhang Qin came to the gate of the Great Black Cave, the tiger was playing with the sun as a fire ball. He ignored his fatigue, held up the long knife and charged towards the tiger. The tiger swallowed the sun into his stomach in a hurry, and swept away Zhang Qin into the sky. Fortunately, Zhang Qin grasped a white cloud, and he lay on it and thought over the way to conquer the tiger. After careful consideration, he decided to get into its stomach to obtain the sun.

When the white cloud fell gradually and touched the top of a pine, Zhan Qin grasped the branch and climbed down the tree. He walked nine days and nights, arrived at the gate of the Great Black Cave. When the violent tiger saw him, it opened its large mouth and wanted to swallow Zhang Qin. He used the long knife and bore the pain to cut a piece of meat from his leg and threw it to the tiger.

The tiger opened its mouth, caught and swallowed the meat into its stomach and looked at Zhang Qin greedily. He cut another piece of meat from his leg again, and threw it to the tiger. It opened its mouth, caught and swallowed the meat into its stomach. It licked again, opened its large mouth, and waited for another piece of meat from Zhang Qin. Zhang Qin saw a good chance, and jumped into the mouth of the tiger. He waved the long knife in its stomach, minced its internal organs, and cut down its main and collateral channels. It gave a loud bellow, fell down and was drown in the Eastern Sea. Zhang Qin chopped and sliced in its stomach. He cut ninety-nine days continuously, cut through its stomach, and climbed out with the sun. He stood on its back, and floated ninety-nine days. Afterwards, he had a pair of wings under his ribs. He leaped into the air from the back of the tiger, and flew into the blue sky. He flew towards the west with wind, and held the red sun with both hands, and prepared to fly back to his hometown. The places which he passed had light and warmth. His blood drops became stars in the sky. Hereafter, the light shone the world.

Since Zhang siblings went to the east, the days of Zhang Village became harder, and they had no food

虎。猛虎一口将肉吞下，舔舔嘴巴，又贪婪地望着张勤。张勤又把腿上的肉割下一块，丢给猛虎。猛虎张口接住，又吞到肚里。猛虎又舔舔嘴巴，张着大口，等待张勤再把肉丢到它嘴里。张勤看好火候，一步跳进老虎嘴里。他在猛虎肚里挥舞长刀，绞碎了猛虎的五脏六腑，割断了猛虎的血管经络。猛虎大吼一声，倒地滚到东海里淹死了。张勤在猛虎肚中，砍呀，刨呀！一刻不停地砍了九十九天，才砍通了老虎的肚皮，举着太阳爬了出来。他站在虎背上，随波漂荡了九十九天。后来，他的肋下长出了一对肉翅膀。他从虎背上往半空一跃，便飞进了蓝天。他乘风西行，双手高举着红彤彤的太阳，准备飞回家乡。所到之处，处处出现了光明和温暖。他身上的血滴变成了满天的繁星。从此，光明洒遍大地。

自从张勤兄妹东去以后，张家村的日子更难熬了，无吃无喝，不到一年，两位老人便相继死去。幺弟张慈埋葬了爹妈，在屋前搭起了一个高台。他爬到高台上，望着东方，日夜不停地喊："哥哥!姐姐! 哥哥……"清明节到了，还不见哥哥、姐姐的踪影。他更难过了，向着东方，不停地又哭又喊："哥哥!姐姐! 哥哥……"喊声在天地间回转。后来，张慈死在屋前的高台上，变成了一只大雄鸡。他忘不了东去的哥哥、姐姐，便飞到石岳山上，满山遍岭的喊叫，寻找亲人。直到现在，石山最高峰玉皇阁前的石皇上，还有一块鸡鸣石，传说就是当时张慈嘶鸣的地方。

张勤在空中听到了弟弟的喊声，日夜不停地往回飞。飞到了南天门，落在银龙洞口。只见当年张智身上的血滴，变成了万蓬杜鹃，肢体变成了千竿翠竹。竹竿可做笛子吹奏山歌，竹皮可做口弦弹唱小调，竹叶可吹奏山

or water. The two old people died consecutively within one year. Zhang Ci, the youngest brother buried the parents, and set up a high platform in front of their house. He climbed on the high platform and looked at the east and cried continuously, "Brothers! Sister! Brothers!..." When Tomb-Sweeping Day approached, he didn't see any trace of his brothers and sister, he felt sadder, he cried and cried towards the east continuously, "Brothers! Sister! Brothers!..." His crying reverberated in the world. Afterwards, Zhang Ci died on the high platform in front of their house and turned into a rooster. He cannot forget his brothers and sister who went to the east, and he flew to Shifou Mountain, cried all over the mountain and looked for his relatives. Till now, there is a piece of crowing stone in front of the Jade Emperor Pavilion at the peak of Shifou Mountain, and it's said that it's the place which Zhang Ci crowed.

Zhang Qin heard the crying of his brother in the air, and he flew back day and night. He arrived at the Southern Heaven Gate and stopped at the gate of the Silver Dragon Cave. The blood drops of Zhang Zhi in that year had turned into azaleas and his body and limbs had changed into green bamboos. The bamboo pole can be used to make flutes, which can play mountain songs, the bamboo skin can be used to make Jew's harp, which can play popular tunes, and the bamboo leaves can play mountain songs… The green bamboo can be used by people to make sticks. Hereafter, people making a pilgrimage to Shifou Mountain will lean on a green bamboo stick when they come back, which is called "Old Man of Bamboo Horse". It's said that people will not feel tired if they lean on "Old Man of Bamboo Horse", because the divine force of Zhang Zhi helps people.

Zhang Qin saw his brother Zhang Zhi, he was so sad while pleased, and couldn't helped crying. His tears turned into a clear spring on the mountain, and people hereafter called it "One Bowl of Water", and people coming and going like to drink the spring water.

Zhang Qin left the Southern Heaven Gate, and flew into the Drilling Sky Slope to look for his sister. When he came to the cave, his sister had turned into a bird, which held the paddy rice, the wheat and the broad bean in her mouth. She sang loudly, "Cuckoo! Cuckoo!" and told the feeling of departure to her brother at the same time. The later generations called the bird into which Zhang Xian changed "Cuckoo". When people heard her crying, they hasted to conduct spring ploughing in fields. Zhan Xian asked about her second brother, Zhang Qin told the fact to her. They had grief and sorrow, and couldn't help crying on each other's shoulder. When they were crying, the cry of Zhang Ci, the youngest brother, was heard. They flew to meet

歌……千竿翠竹给人们作手杖。后来，凡朝石砬山的人，回时都要挂一根翠竹手杖，人们称为"竹马老头"。据说，挂着"竹马老头"，走路爬山不会累，因为有张智的神力扶助着人们。

张勤见到张智弟弟，又伤心，又喜欢，禁不住泪水长流。他的眼泪汇成了山上的一眼清泉，后人把这泉叫作"一碗水"，来往行人都喜欢饮用这泉水。

张勤离了南天门，飞到钻天坡寻找妹妹。到了石洞，只见妹妹已变成一只小鸟，口衔稻谷、小麦、蚕豆种。一边高唱"布谷!布谷！"一边向哥哥诉说离情。后人把张贤变的小鸟叫做"布谷雀"。只要一听到她的叫声，人们就赶快下田春耕。张贤问起二哥，张勤如实地告诉了妹妹。两人悲痛交加，不由抱头痛哭。两兄妹正在啼哭，传来了幺弟张慈的喊声。兄妹二人飞上前去迎接弟弟，三人在一个土坡上见了面。三人相聚，悲喜交集，不由抱头痛哭。三人的泪水淌成了河，把土坟冲成了千曲百弯。

后人把兄妹三人的泪水冲成的大阱叫作清泪阱。人们上下石岳山就从阱中来往，后来走出了一条路，便把这条路叫作"九转十八望乡路"。

后来，弟弟张慈回到家里照顾爹妈的坟山。张勤和张贤兄妹飞遍天下，给人们送去光明、温暖和粮食。张贤怕人们误了农时，一到春耕前，她便飞遍天涯海角，高叫着："布谷！布谷！"催促人们播种。张勤怕么弟一人在家孤单，一听见雄鸡啼叫，就召集张勤兄妹四人，每年农历三月初十，在石山银龙洞相会一次。人们忘不了他兄妹四人的功劳；也忘不了牟伽佗祖师开辟鹤庆的丰功。所以，每年农历三月，各村各寨的人们，端着五谷，

their youngest brother. They met with each other on a slope. The siblings were pleased and sad and cried on one other's shoulder. The tears of the three persons turned into the river, and flushed the tombs into thousands of gulves.

The later generations called the well which was flushed by the tears of the siblings "Clear Tear Well". People climbed Shifou Mountain, and came to the well, a road was formed, and they called the road "Road of Nine Turns and Eighteen Looks towards Hometown".

Afterwards, the brother Zhang Ci returned home to take care of the tombs of their parents. Zhang Qin and Zhang Xian flew over the world, and sent the light, the warmth and the grains to people. Zhang Xian feared that people would miss farming season, she flew everywhere before the spring ploughing, and cried loudly, "Cuckoo! Cuckoo!" to haste people to sow seeds. Zhang Qin feared that the youngest brother would be lonely at home, so he asked the four siblings to meet with each other in the Silver Dragon Cave in the mountain on lunar March 10th when he heard the crowing of the rooster. People didn't forget the merits of the four siblings as well as the heroic deed of the master Mou Gatuo who created Heqing. Therefore, people from various villages carried the five cereals, hometown water, fried broad beans, pilgrimage cakes and liquor, played three-stringed instrument, sang mountain songs and came to Shifou Mountain to sacrifice to the master Mou Gatuo and the four siblings, including Zhang Qin, Zhang Zhi, Zhang Xian and Zhang Ci[①].

After arriving at the top of the mountain, people came to the cave of the master and grasped a handful soil to home, threw it to fields, which can bless timely wind and rain. They came to the slope and picked up a stone, brought it home and put it on the roof, which can avoid wind and fire disasters. Azaleas which were plucked at the Southern Heaven Gate can bless peace of the whole family, even a bamboo brought home can avoid monsters and expel evil spirits. People worship them every year to commemorate the heroic deeds of the four siblings of Zhang and the Divine Mother of the Five Cereals who look for light and happiness for human beings. The convention has been passed down from the ancient to modern times, and there is a local saying that "there is a March 3rd every year, and people make a pilgrimage to Shifou Mountain on March 15th;

背着家乡水、炒蚕豆。做些朝山粑粑，带上烧酒，吹着笛子，弹着三弦，唱着山歌来到石岳山上祭供牟伽佗祖师和张勤、张智、张贤、张慈四人[①]。

人们到了山顶之后，会去祖师洞抓一把泥土带回家，丢进田里，可以保佑风调雨顺。到山坡上拣个石头拿回家放在屋顶上，可以免除风火二灾。在南天门采摘的杜鹃花是保佑全家平安的，甚至砍一根竹子带回家，都可以避魔逐邪。人们年年都去祭拜他们，怀念张氏四兄妹和五谷神婆为人类寻找

①Collection of Chinese Folk Customs and Sources (Volume of Holidays and Seasons), pp141—148.

①雪犁 等主编，《中华民俗源流集成（节日岁时卷）》，甘肃人民出版社，1994年，第141—148页

光明和幸福的英雄事迹。这个习俗从古至今，沿袭不绝，当地的俗话说"年年有个三月三，三月十五朝石岙山；四乡八寨人聚会，热闹不过石岙山"。

对于湖北的土家族来说，三月三和蛇妖有关，而且在三月三那天，必须用糯米粑粑将磨眼塞住，才能保平安。当地有一句俗语，"三月三，蛇出山；九月九，蛇钻孔。"

传说，从前土家山寨有两条成精的毒蛇，每年农历三月三出洞，到处危害人畜，直到九月九才回洞。有年农历三月初三，玉皇大帝见一户人家有毒蛇兴妖作怪，便派神仙下凡斩妖。蛇妖见大事不好，赶忙钻进磨眼里。神仙顺手用糯米粑粑塞住磨眼，毒蛇再也出不来了。

从此，每年农历三月初三这天，土家人就用糯米粑粑塞住磨眼，可免遭蛇咬。

the villagers from everywhere get together and Shifou Mountain is so lively."

As for Tujia people of Hubei, March 3rd was related to snake monsters, and people must use glutinous rice cakes to block the eye of the grinder in order to bless peace. There is a local saying, "Snakes come out of mountains on March 3rd; and they climb into pores on September 9th."

It was said that there were two poisonous snakes which became sprits in the village of Tujia people, they came out of the cave on lunar March 3rd to harm people and animals everywhere, and they came back to the cave on September 9th. The Jade Emperor saw poisonous snakes making troubles in a household, and assigned an immortal to come to the earth to cut the snake. The snake monster saw the imminent disaster, and climbed into the eye of the grinder in a hurry. The immortal used the glutinous rice cake to block the eye of the grinder and the poisonous snake cannot come out any more.

Hereafter, Tujia people use glutinous rice cakes to block eyes of grinders to avoid the bites of snakes on lunar March 3rd every year.

Zhuang people of Guangxi don't hold temple fair, but sing songs to meet friends on March 3rd, they sing songs three days and nights, and their songs fly over the Red River and drift in the air over the Xi River. In lunar March, Zhuang people in Longhong and Cifu at the two banks of Panyang River of Guangong Community of Bama City come to fields to set up song sheds, young men and women are meticulously dressed, young women wear clothes dyed and weaved by themselves, young men are spirited up after cleaning, young women dye red eggs and steam five-colored glutinous rice, put glutinous rice in small cloth bags and eggs on delicate silk bags ,then they go to streets to participate in the folk song fair.

广西的壮族人民在三月三的时候，可不是举行庙会了，而是以歌会友，唱上三天三夜，歌声飞过红河，飘荡在西江上空。每年农历的三月，在巴马城关公社盘阳河两岸的龙洪，赐福一带，壮族同胞们到野外搭歌棚，姑娘小伙儿们都精心装扮，姑娘们穿上自己染织的衣服，小伙子们梳洗得精神抖擞，姑娘们染红鸡蛋，蒸五色糯饭，把糯饭装进小布袋里，把蛋装进玲珑丝网袋里，到街上赶歌圩去。

巴马的三月三歌节，也是有动人的故事，有两种说法。

(一)古时有一对青年男女相恋，父母反对他们成婚，他们在二月三十日晚跑上山坡，爬上枫树，痛哭殉情。两人鲜血染满枫树和树下的红兰草。到三月初三那天，人们上山，发现他们，深表同情。于是找枫叶和红兰草染糯米饭，唱歌纪念，代代相传，形成歌节。

(二)唐代，壮家出了刘三姐，三月初三那天为财主害死。后人为纪念歌仙，于三月初三、四、五唱歌三天，形成歌圩。

歌圩现场，男女青年都是一对对地走进歌唱，以村屯为单位，特别是姑娘们，统一着装，非常吸引大家的注意力。对歌的时候，你问我答，此落彼起，兴致勃勃的时候可以连唱几天都不停。通过对歌的形式，青年男女们互相认识而结为夫妻，这也

There are two sayings for the moving stories of March 3rd Song Festival in Bama.

(1) A pair of young man and woman fell in love with each other in the ancient times, but their parents objected them to marry. They came to the slope, climbed on the ample tree, and cried to death for love on February 30th, the ample tree and the red orchid under it were stained with their blood. People climbed the mountain, found them and showed sympathy deeply on March 3rd. They used maple leaves and red orchid to dye glutinous rice, and sang songs to commemorate the couple for generations, and the song fair has been formed.

(2) The Third Sister of Liu from Zhuang people was forced by the rich people to die on March 3rd in the Tang Dynasty. The later generations sang songs on March 3rd, 4th and 5th and formed the song fair to commemorate her.

Couples of young men and women enter the song fair to sing songs in group of village, especially young women wearing uniform cloths, which can attract attention of people. When they sing in antiphonal style, one asks questions and the other answers them, when one starts singing, another joins in, they can sing songs for days continuously with great enthusiasm. Through the form of singing in antiphonal style, young men and women know each other and marry, which makes the song fair have more romantic feel[1].

Zhuang people of Guangnan, Yunnan celebrate March 3rd in another form. Young women are called Leshao, wear angled cloth scarf, short covering, long skirt, embroidered shoes and silver ornaments, and go to streets with companions to sing songs with young men in antiphonal style, which is called "Going to Flower Street" locally. There is an exquisite story about Going to Flower Street on March 3rd:

让歌会具有了更多浪漫主义的色彩[1]。

云南广南的壮族，在三月初三又是另外一种庆祝形式。在当地，女青年被称为勒少，头顶翘角布巾，穿上短衣长裙和绣花鞋，戴上银饰，和同伴们到街上去与男青年对歌，这在当地被称为"赶花街"。三月初三赶花街，还有一个奇巧的故事呢：

[1]Records of Customs of Guangxi Minorities, ed, by Guangxi Ethnic and Folk Literature Research Office of Nanning Teachers College/ Oct. 1984, Version 1, p9.

[1]南宁师范学院广西民族民间文学研究室编，《广西少数民族风情录》，1984年10月第1版，第9页

古代，有个勒少，叫狄娃。她呀，没有一个勒少的长相有她那么漂亮，没有一个勒少绣的花有她绣的那么美丽，没有一个勒少炒的菜有她炒的那么甜香，没有一个勒少唱的歌有她唱的那么动听！她是勒少心中的月亮，是勒冒心中的太阳，说多好，就有多好！

狄娃样样都好，但她的命运却不好。

每天，到狄娃家提亲的媒人排成队，她家也不答应，每晚，来找狄娃唱歌的勒冒一个接一个，她父亲一个也不喜欢，却偏偏将她答应嫁给一个长相丑、心狠毒、年纪大的财主做小老婆！狄娃知道这事后，哭着跪在父亲脚下，请求退掉这门婚事，她父亲不仅不依，反而与那财主合谋，将婚期定在三月间，逼着她天天赶做嫁妆，她哭着跪在母亲脚下，求母亲帮忙，母亲说她作不了主，她哭着走去求阿哥，叫阿哥劝说父

In the ancient times, there was a young woman named Diwa, she was the prettiest young woman, she can embroider the most beautiful flowers , she can fry the most delicious dishes, and she can sing the most fair-sounding songs. She was the moon of young women, and was the sun of young men. She was very nice and fair.

Diwa was good at everything, but her fate wasn't good.

Everyday, a long queue of matchmakers went to the house of Diwa to propose a marriage, but her father didn't accept anyone; in the evening, plenty of young men came to sing with her. Her father didn't like anyone, but promised to marry her to an old rich man as a concubine. When knowing it, Diwa cried and knelt at the feet of her father, and begged him to cancel the marriage, but her father didn't comply with her words, plotted with the rich man and fixed the marriage in March, forced her to make dowry, she cried and knelt at the feet of her mother, asked help from her, but her mother said that she couldn't help her; she cried and came to her brother, asked him to persuade their father, but her brother said that he could do nothing for her. She cried everyday until she had no more tears to shed, and her eyes were swollen.

亲，阿哥说他无能为力。
急得她天天哭天号地，哭
干了眼泪，哭肿了双眼！

One night, she was worried, turned and tossed in bed, and couldn't sleep because the marriage was approaching. After a while, she got up, wore her favorite clothes, skirt, silver chain and bracelets, walked out of her house stealthily in the still of night, and walked towards the direction of sunrise in the moon light.

一天夜间，眼看婚期
就要到了，她心如刀绞，
在床上翻来覆去．老是睡
不着觉，过了一会，她翻
身起床，将她最喜爱的衣
裳、裙子穿上，将最喜爱
的银链，银镯戴上，趁着
夜深人静，悄悄走出家
门，踏着月光，朝着太阳
出来的方向走去。

Diwa left home to escape from her marriage.

狄娃出走逃婚了。

She escaped from her house, quickened her steps, walked towards villages, mountains and forests because she feared that her father would know her trace.

逃出了家，狄娃怕父
亲知道她的去向，就加快
脚步，有村寨往哪里走，
哪里山大林密往哪里钻。

She walked without stop, climbed many mountains and crossed several forests, and arrived at a mountain when a rooster crowed a second time. She felt so tired at this moment.

狄娃走呀走，不知翻
过几架山，也不知穿过几
片森林，鸡叫第二遍时，
来到一架大山上。此时，
她感到又累又困，

Under a tree, she laid her back against the tree and closed her eyes to sleep.

在一棵大树下，背靠
大树，闭起眼睛睡觉。

刚一闭眼，狄娃就睡着了。不多一会，她做了一个梦，梦见她走到一个山清水秀的寨子，站在一棵万年青树下，和一个叫那多的勒冒对歌。

那个那多呀，黑黑的眉毛，大大的眼睛，高高的鼻子，厚厚的嘴唇，下巴上有颗黑疙，显得很漂亮。他唱的歌呀，比画眉鸟唱的还动听，比泉水还要清甜！

狄娃看了那多的长相，听了那多唱的歌，心想，找着那多这样的勒冒做丈夫，就称心如意了。于是，她用歌声主动向那多表达了爱慕之情，一边唱，一边向那多走拢。

狄娃刚走到那多面前，一个男人咚的一声跳到她面前，举起手中的刀，就要杀她。

那多见到这情景，飞起一脚，将那男人手中的刀踢落在地上，狄娃一看，要杀她的那男人不是别人，正是要娶她做小老

When she closed her eyes, she fell asleep. After a while, she had a dream, dreamed that she walked into a village with a beautiful view, stood under an evergreen tree, and sang songs with a young man named Naduo.

Naduo had black eyebrows, big eyes, high nose and thick lips, and there was a black mole on his chin, which was so pretty. His songs were more fair-sounding than a throstle and sweeter than spring water.

Looking at the face of Naduo, and listening to his songs, Diwa thought, "I will be glad to have a young man like Naduo as my husband." Therefore, she sang songs to declare her heart actively, and walked towards Naduo.

When Diwa walked towards of Naduo, a man jumped in front of her with a knife in his hand, and was going to kill her.

Seeing the scene, Naduo kicked the knife off the hand of the man, Diwa saw the man who was going to kill her was the rich man, he wanted to marry her as a concubine, and she was angry and cried.

婆的财主，她气得哇哇大哭。

Naduo pointed at Diwa and asked the rich man, "Why will you kill this young woman?"

那多指着狄娃问财主："你为哪样要杀这个勒少？"

The rich man looked at Naduo and said, "Wow, it's Naduo! I tell you, you shall not call Diwa, she is the wife I am going to marry!"

财主看了那多几眼，说"哟，原来是那多呀！告诉你少叫狄娃，是我要娶的老婆！"

Naduo said loudly, "Let alone the wife who you are going to marry, even the maid, you shall not kill her!"

那多听了，大声说："别说她是你要讨的老婆，就算丫头，你也不能杀嘛！"

The rich man pointed at Diwa and said, "She escape from the marriage, and isn't willing to marry me!"

财主指着狄娃，说："她逃婚，她不愿嫁我！"

Naduo looked at the rich man and said coldly, "You are so cruel and ugly, how will she marry you?"

那多打量财主几眼，冷冰冰地说："你心毒手狠，而且那么丑陋，她怎么会嫁你！"

The rich man thought that he wasn't the competitor of Naduo, cannot outspeak Naduo, so he winked his eyes, and turned away. After walking several steps, he grasped the knife on the ground, turned back and killed Naduo with the knife.

财主见自己不是那多的对手，又说不赢那多，转动几下眼睛，就走开了。他走了几步，抓起地上的刀，呼地转回身，几刀将那多杀翻在地。

狄娃见到这惨景，大叫一声，啪的倒在那多尸体上。

随着这一声大叫，狄娃惊醒了。她睁开眼，见太阳已挂在树梢，自己还靠在大树下，才知道她做了一个噩梦！狄娃站起身来，见山下有个百花掩映的村寨，肚子又饿，就朝山下走去，准备找碗饭吃，歇歇气，再逃到远方去。

狄娃走到那个村寨时，正逢街子天，男女老少在街上，卖的卖，买的买，非常热闹。

说奇真奇，说巧真巧！狄娃走到街头，正想进街时，见万年青树下有个龙潭，顿觉口渴，头又有点晕，就走到龙潭边捧水喝喝了几口水，又见龙潭水清澈明净，她的倒影投在水面，连眼睛鼻子都看得清楚，就对着水面，梳妆打扮起来。

恰在这时，水面上呈

Seeing the miserable scene, Diwa cried loudly and threw herself on the body of Naduo.

With the cry, Diwa woke up. She opened her eyes, saw the sun hanging at the tree top, she was still lying against the tree, and knew that she dreamed a nightmare. She stood up and saw a village which was surrounded by a hundred flowers at the foot of the mountain, and she was hungry, walked down the mountain, and was going to eat something, had a rest and then escaped afar.

When Diwa walked into the village, it was the day of going to street, people crowded in the street, some people were selling, some people were buying, and it was very lively.

What a coincidence it was! When Diwa wanted to go into the street at the entrance, there was a dragon pool under an evergreen tree, she felt thirsty and dizzy, then walked to the pool and drank water. The pool water was clean and clear, her shadow was cast on the water surface, her eyes and nose could be seen clearly, so she looked at the water surface and made up.

At this moment, there was a shadow of a young

man on the water surface, who stood together with her happily.

The young man in the water had black brows, big eyes, high nose, thick lips, and a black mole on the chin. The appearance was the same as that in her dream last night.

When Diwa looked at the shadow of Naduo who she dreamed in the water, she lost her consciousness for the reason of fatigue, or hunger, or loss of sleep. She stared at the shadow of Naduo in the water for a long time, and asked, "Brother, are you Naduo?"

Naduo smiled and answered gently, "Yes!"

Wasn't Naduo in the dream killed by the rich man? She rubbed her eyes and asked Naduo in the water, "Are you really Naduo?"

Naduo answered gently with smile, "Yes!"

Oh! Naduo didn't die really! Diwa was pleased and laughed.

现出一个勒冒的影子，笑盈盈地和她站在一起。

呀！那水中的勒冒，黑黑的眉毛，大大的眼睛，高高的鼻子，厚厚的嘴唇，下巴上有颗黑痣。这长相，和她昨晚梦见的那多一模一样！

狄娃不知是累，是饿，还是觉没有睡足，她看着映在水中的梦中见到的那多的影子，像做梦一般，失去了神志。她痴呆呆地对着水中那多的影子看了半天，问："阿哥，你叫那多吗？"

那多笑眯眯地轻声回答"是。"

咦，梦中的那多不是被财主杀死了吗？狄娃揉了揉眼睛问水中的那多："你真是那多吗？"

那多又笑眯眯地轻声回答："是。"

哟，那多当真没有死呢！狄娃乐了，笑了。

这一乐一笑，狄娃恢复了神志，马上对水中那多的影子问："那多哥，我见到你，昨晚在梦中，现在在水中，你到底在什么地方呀？"

那多仍然笑眯眯地轻声回答："狄娃呀，我现在正站在你身边呢。"

狄娃侧身一看，那多当真站在她身边啦！她红着脸，喘着气对那多说："那多哥，我还在做梦吧？"

那多说，"我都站在你身边了，你怎么说还是做梦呢！狄娃呀，我每晚都到你家找你唱歌，难道你忘记了我啦？昨晚，我来找你唱歌，见你出走，逃婚了，我就尾追你，走到这里来了。狄娃，你说过，你爱我，我也说过，我爱你。难道这些你都忘记了吗？"

狄娃说："怎能忘呢？我逃婚时，本来想去你家，同你结成夫妻，

The happiness and laugh made Diwa regain her consciousness, and she asked the shadow of Naduo in the water immediately, "Brother Naduo, I saw you in my dream last night, and you are in the water now! Where are you on earth?"

Naduo answered gently with smiled, "Diwa, I am standing beside you!"

Diwa turned around and saw Naduo standing beside her! Her face turned red, she gasped and said to Naduo, "Brother Naduo, am I still dreaming?"

Naduo said, "I am standing beside you. How can you dream? Diwa, I went to your house to sing songs with you every night, do you forget me? Last night, I came to sing songs with you and saw you escaping from the marriage, so I pursued you, and came here. Diwa, you said that you loved me, and I said that I loved you. Did you forget everything?"

Diwa said, "How can I forget the words? When I escaped from the marriage, I wanted to go to your house, and married you, but I didn't know where

your house was, where your village was. I feared that I would implicate you, bring suffers to you, so I arrived here. When I slept last night, I dreamed that I sang songs with you, and the rich man who wanted to marry me killed you!"

When hearing her words, Naduo was pleased. Hereafter, Diwa and Naduo loved each other, and they lived in harmony and grew old together.

但不知道你家在哪方，住哪个寨子。又怕我连累了你，使你遭难，才遇到这儿来的。昨晚我睡觉时，都还梦见同你唱歌，梦见要娶我的那个财主杀你呢！"

那多听了这番话，乐了！此后狄娃那多恩恩爱爱，万分和睦，直到白头偕老。

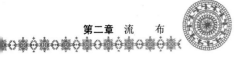

第三章

风俗

三三令节重厨房，口味新调又一桩。地米菜和鸡蛋煮，十分耐饱十分香。

——清·叶调元《汉口竹枝词》

　　流杯、流卵、流枣、吃青精饭、踏青、歌会等等，这些都是民间三月三的习俗，只不过不同的地方有各自的地方特色。城镇儿童多于此日放纸鸢，以表凌云之志。人们随身携带葱蒜，在家门上插桃树枝，用来避邪。

Chapter There

Customs

The festival of March 3rd attaches importance to kitchen, and there are many new tastes. Eggs are boiled with shepherd's purse, which are very hunger-resistant and delicious.

——Ye Diaoyuan's *Poem of Hankou Bamboo Branches* in the Qing Dynasty

Floating goblets, eggs and dates, eating green fine rice, spring outing and song fair are the folk conventions on March 3rd, and different places have different characteristics. Township children fly kites to express their great aspirations. People carry onion and garlic on them, and erect peach branches on doors to avoid evil spirits.

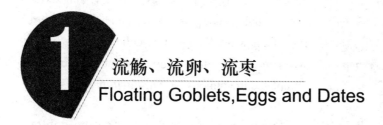

流觞、流卵、流枣
Floating Goblets,Eggs and Dates

Since the Pre-Qin, men of letters have had the convention of floating goblets beside streams on March 3rd. The games of winding water and floating goblets are usually held in the river channel or beside the stream. After holding the Fuxi ceremony, they are seated on the ground, put the goblets upstream, and let them drift down the water. When the goblet stops in front of someone, he takes the goblet, drinks it, composes a poem or plays other programs impromptu.

On March 3rd of Yonghe's 9th Year in the Eastern Jin Dynasty (353 AD), Wang Xizhi, the great calligrapher met his friends in the Orchid Pavilion in Shanyin of Kuaiji (Shaoxing of Zhejiang today), his relatives and friends held the game of winding water and floating goblets after the ceremony of Xiuqi, one had to compose a poem and drink wine if a goblet turned or stopped in front of

先秦以来，文人墨客就有三月三在溪边流觞的习俗。曲水流觞这种游戏通常是在河渠或溪边举行，人们举行祓禊仪式之后，席地而坐，在上游放置酒杯，让酒杯顺水而下，当酒杯停在谁的面前，谁就取杯饮酒，赋诗一首或即兴表演其他节目。

东晋永和九年（353年）的三月初三，大书法家王羲之与朋友在会稽山阴（今浙江绍兴）的兰亭相聚，修禊之后与亲朋举行流觞曲水的游戏，酒杯在谁面前打转或停下，谁就要即兴赋诗并饮酒。据

史载，四十二人饮酒咏诗，有十一人各成诗两篇，有十六人作不出诗来，被罚酒三杯。王羲之将大家的诗句收集起来，并挥笔作序，乘兴而书，一挥即就，完成了天下闻名的《兰亭集序》。

在三月三当天，除了流觞的习俗，还有流枣流卵的活动。三月三有祓除不祥的仪式，被称之为祓禊，而流枣的活动是祓禊保平安的延续，只不

him. According to the historical record, forty-two people drank wine and composed poems, eleven people made two poems respectively, and sixteen people couldn't compose poems and were fined three goblets of wine. Wang Xizhi collected their poems, wrote the preface and calligraphy in high spirits, and completed the famous *Orchid Pavilion Preface*.

Besides the convention of floating goblets, there are the activities of floating dates and eggs on March 3rd. The convention of getting rid of ill omen is called Baxi, and the activity of floating dates is the extension of Baxi to get rid of evils and bless peace, which is endowed more contents related to vitality and reproduction. Du Du in the Eastern Han

Dynasty wrote in *Baxi Poem* that "floating dates blush water and pouring wine make the river have the strong taste." Zhang Xie in the Jin Dynasty wrote that "float white eggs in water, and pour wine with dregs into the river", and Liu Yun wrote in one of *Two Five-Character and Seven-Character Poems Responding to the Emperor's Poems on Cold Food* that, "The eggs float on the waves, the orchids are auspicious and fragrant, the pheasants flying in ridges, and the timely wheat grows up."

The activities of floating dates and eggs are related to the ancient concept of reproduction and praying for sons. Before understanding life and reproduction clearly, people thought that life came from heavenly endowment, and there were many legends of "pregnancy from sense". For example, the *Book of Rites: Monthly Instructions* recorded that, "Spring was the season for Xuan Birds to come. When Xuan Birds came, it's time to sacrifice to the Matchmaking God. The emperor came to the suburbs with all concubines in the imperial carriages. They brought arrows and bows and put them in front of the Matchmaking God." Zheng Xuan noted that, "Gaoxin was from the remaining egg of a Xuan Bird, Song Jian ate it and delivered Qi. The latter kings thought the matchmaking official was auspicious, so set up a temple for him. Matchmaker was treated as a god. " That is to say, Song Jian swallowed the remaining egg of

过被赋予了更多与生命力和繁殖有关的内容。东汉杜笃《祓禊赋》写道"浮枣绛水，醋酒醲川。" 晋张协《洛禊赋》云："浮素卵以蔽水，洒玄醪于中河"，宋代刘筠《奉和圣制寒食五七言二首》其一中说："波浮素卵祥兰馥，垒戏名羣瑞麦新。"

流枣流卵的活动与古代的生育观念和祈子文化有关。在尚未明晓生命繁衍的原理之前，人们认为生命来自于天赐，甚至在远古神话中往往都有众多"受感而孕"的传说。例如，《礼记·月令》记载："仲春之月，是月也，玄鸟至。至之日，以大牢祠于高禖。天子亲往，后妃帅九嫔御，乃礼天子所御。带以弓韣，授以弓矢，于高禖之前。"郑玄注曰："高辛氏之出，玄鸟遗卵，娀简吞之而生契，后王以为媒官嘉祥，而立其祠焉。变媒言禖，神之也。" 也就是说，娀简吞玄鸟遗卵而生子。这种神话在《诗经》中比比皆是，玄鸟的出现意味着主人孕育子嗣的可能性，所以玄鸟又与繁衍生育有关，在春天玄鸟来临时，人们在野外举行祈子活动，而三月三又是这个迎玄鸟活动的主要时间。并且古代的人们还相信"交感巫术"，也就是吃下鸡蛋就会怀孕的观念，所以在三月三的时候，妇女们在河边将鸡蛋放置于水中，以期望获得神力来帮助孕育。此后，三月三用荠菜炒鸡蛋的习俗也是这个观念的变体。

a Xuan Bird and bore the son. *The Book of Songs* was full of this kind of legend, and the appearance of Xuan Bird meant the possibility of a master of begetting a son, so Xuan Bird was related to reproduction and fertility. When spring and Xuan Bird come, people hold the activity of praying for sons in wild fields, and March 3rd is the main time to the activity of meeting Xuan Bird. In the ancient times, people believed in "sympathetic magic", i.e. the concept that a person eating an egg can be pregnant. Therefore, people put eggs beside a river in order to expect that they can obtain superhuman power to help pregnancy and fertility. Hereafter, the convention of frying shepherd's purse with eggs on March 3rd became a variable of the convention.

2 插柳踏青
Wearing Willow and Spring Outing

People have the activity of spring outing and wearing willow circle for Tomb-Sweeping Festival now, which is one of the conventions of Shangsi Festival on March 3rd. Since the Tang Dynasty, people have had the convention of wearing willow circle or erecting willow, and *Miscellaneous Morsels from Youyang* records that, "Emperor Zhongzong of the Tang Dynasty awarded willow circles to his courtiers, wearing them can avoid scorpion venom." *The Book of the Tang: Biography of Lishi* has the saying that "willow circles can get rid of diseases." *Records of a Year's Events in Beijing: Tomb-Sweeping Festival* writes that, "As for wearing willow on Tomb-Sweeping Festival, Emperor Gaozong of the Tang Dynasty awarded one willow circle to each courtier beside the Wei River at the ceremony of getting rid of evil spirits

现在清明节的时候，人们都有外出踏青、头戴柳圈的活动，实际上这个活动是三月三上巳节的习俗之一。从唐代起，就已经有戴柳圈或插柳的习俗了，《酉阳杂俎》记载："唐中宗三月三日，赐侍臣细柳圈，带之可免虿毒。"《唐书·李适传》也有"细柳圈辟病"的说法。清代的《燕京岁时记·清明》中说："至清明戴柳青，乃唐高宗三月三日被褉于渭水之隅，赐群臣柳圈各一，谓戴之可免虿毒。"由此可以看

113

出，上巳节虽然已经和清明、寒食节合并了，但其习俗也保留下来，流传至今。

on March 3rd, and it's said that wearing willow can avoid scorpion venom." From the above, we can see that Shangsi Festival has integrated with Tomb-Sweeping Festival and Cold Food Festival, and the convention has been kept and spread till now.

3 饮食习俗
Diet Customs

There are different diet conventions on March 3rd in profound diet cultures including black rice, clear fine rice, killing fish and glutinous cake. Qichun people use rice to make cake, whose name is "eating head of ghost", meaning dispelling evil spirits and blessing peace; there is a curious coincidence, people eat fried corns on March 3rd in some places, and it's said that "eyes of ghosts are fried", so that they cannot find houses of masters; common people in some places make dough balls to eat, which are called "heads of ghosts". People boil eggs in bovine urine and let their children eat, and it's said that a hundred diseases can be avoided.

乌饭、清精饭、杀鱼、糯米粑粑，在博大精深的华夏饮食文化中，三月三的饮食习俗各有不同。蕲春人用大米做菜粑，名曰"吃鬼头"，意思是驱邪保佑平安；无独有偶，还有一些地方在三月三的时候炒包谷粒吃，据说可以"炸鬼眼睛"，让小鬼们找不到主家；还有一些地方的老百姓做疙瘩吃，也是说"鬼头"。还有一些地方用牛尿煮鸡蛋给小伢吃，据说可免百病。

清精饭，又名青精饭，这一习俗甚至可以追溯到上古时期。《岁时广记》卷十五记载："彭祖云：大宛有青精饭先生，青灵真人霍山道士邓伯元者，受青精饭法。"梁时甚至在《登真隐诀》出现了专门的"太极真人青精干石食迅饭法"，这是道家研制出来的辟谷方剂。后来，老百姓也逐渐食用青精饭，唐代大诗人杜甫《赠李白》写道："岂无青精饭，使我颜色好。"张贲《以青食迅饭分送袭美鲁望因成一绝》写："谁屑琼瑶事青食迅，旧传名品出华阳。应宜仙子胡麻拌，因送刘郎与阮郎。"这些诗句都是当时制作食用青精饭习俗的见证。

Clear fine rice is also called green fine rice, and this convention can be even traced back to the ancient times. Volume 15 of *Extensive Records of Seasons* writes that, "Ancestor Peng said that there was a master of grass fine rice in Dawan. Deng Boyuan, who was Green and Holy Immortal 'and Huo Mountain Taoist, taught the method of green fine rice". Liang Shi wrote the special method of green fine dry stone instant rice of the Great Ultimate Immortal in *Secret Formulas for Attaining Perfection*, and this was the recipe developed by Taoism to refrain from eating grain. Hereafter, common people began to eat green vegetable rice. Du Fu, the great poet in the Tang Dynasty, wrote in *For Li Bai* that, "I was so pleased with green vegetable rice." Zhang Ben wrote in *A Poem on Sending Instant Green Rice to Ximei and Luwang* that, "People don't care about exquisite things but eat green fine rice, and its fame is popular outside Huayang. It's proper to mix it with flaxes, so I sent it to Mr. Liu and Mr. Ruan." These poems prove the convention of making and eating black vegetable rice at that time.

Black rice grass and stems and leaves of Adinandra millettii are mashed up and added into rice which is soaked in the juice, and then is steamed, so it is called green fine rice. Some places in Guangdong have the similar making method, and people soak glutinous rice in liquid of tender leaves of green maple and Sapium sebiferum and eat it after they steam it. This is similar to the method of making green fine rice in the Song Dynasty. From ancient times to the Five Dynasties and the two Song Dynasties, the method had become more and more exquisite. According to Liang Kejia's Volume 14 of *Records of the Three Mountains from the Chunxi Reign* in the Song Dynasty, it recorded green rice for Shangsi Festival, "Southern candelilla are evergreen in winter and summer, people take and mash up its leaves, soak rice in the liquid, dye it into green, and eat a bowl per day, and can enjoy longevity. It is called Shangsi green rice, and Fujian conventions follow it. " After the Yuan Dynasty, people ate green fine rice in Cold Food Festival, "People will not be bored of green fine rice for additional meals, and White Stone Sheep can bear being boiled". However, Lin Hong pointed out in *Mountain Diet* that folk green fine rice differed from green fine rice eaten by immortals in terms of formulation and making methods, the latter added greenstone grease and foxtail millet seeds, and pills were made to refrain from eating grain. After the Ming and Qing Dynasties, green fine rice was made on the day sacrificing to Land Gods in many places in the south and it had been spread to minorities. Li

青精饭是用乌饭草和杨桐茎叶捣碎后拌入粳米中，使得渍汁浸粳米，再蒸熟而成。广东有些地方至今还有类似做法，将青枫、乌桕嫩叶浸泡后把糯米放入胶液中蒸熟食用。这和宋代制作青精饭的方法差不多。上古时期的做法到五代和两宋之后，做法越来越精致。据宋梁克家《淳熙三山志》（卷四十）记载上巳节所食的青饭："南烛木冬夏常青，取其叶，捣碎，渍米为饭，染成绀青之色，日进一合，可以延年，今上巳青饭，闽俗效之。" 元代以后，寒食节也食青精饭，"加餐未厌青精饭，烂煮那无白石羊。" 但是，林洪在《山家清供》中指出民间青精饭及仙家服食的青精石饭在配方制法上的差异，后者还要加入青石脂及青精米，制成药丸食用以辟谷。明清以后，南方许多地区在社日的时候制作青精饭，还传播

117

到少数民族当中，清代李调元《南越笔记》卷十三说"今苏罗人每以社日为青精饭相馈。"

Diaoyuan in the Qing Dynasty wrote in Volume 13 of *Notes on Lingnan* that, "Suluo people eat green fine rice on the day of sacrificing to Land Gods every year."

畲族百姓在三月三的时候家家户户做乌饭，过"乌饭节"。乌饭是用乌稔树的叶子浸泡出汁液，然后再将糯米放在里面浸泡，最后蒸熟。乌饭德颜色是蓝乌色，香甜可口，有时还可以加点猪油来炒，更加美味，香气扑鼻。

Households of She people make black rice on March 3rd to celebrate "Black Rice Festival". Leaves of oriental blueberry are soaked into juice, and then glutinous rice is soaked in it, and then black rich is steamed. The color of black rice is black and blue, and it tastes sweet and delicious, sometimes lard oil is added to fry it, which makes it more delicious and fragrant.

It's said that the origin of black rice is related to Lei Wanxing, who was the hero of She people in the Tang Dynasty. Lei Wanxing led She soldiers to resist control and management of local authorities, and they were besieged by the armies of the imperial court. When they had no grains, they found fruits of oriental blueberry in the forest, which can be edible. Therefore, She soldiers plucked fruits of oriental blueberry, and laid the foundation for the final victory. After the victory, Lei Wanxing ordered to boil glutinous rice with leaves of oriental blueberry, and the glutinous rice which was made had the same color as fruits of oriental blueberry but was fragrant, so Lei Wanxing was very glad. She people go out to pluck leaves of oriental blueberry and make black rice on March 3rd in order to commemorate the heroic deeds of Lei Wanxing.

Besides its relation to Lei Wanxing, the hero of She people, there is another legend about black rice:

Long long ago, the harvest was bad because of ant and insect pest and increased rental and tax of the mountain masters in March, chimney smokes of households of She people disappeared, and the abominable mountain master robbed rice seeds. People had no grains, they dug wild vegetables to allay their hunger, and there were no seed to sow.

乌饭的由来据说与唐代的畲族英雄雷万兴有关。雷万兴带着畲族士兵反抗官府的管制，被朝廷的军队围在大山之中，粮草都没有了的时候，他们在树林里找到乌稔树的果实，发现这种果实可以充饥。于是，畲族士兵们纷纷摘采乌稔树果实，为最后的胜利奠定了基础。胜利以后，雷万兴下令将乌稔树的叶子用来煮糯米饭，做出来的糯米饭也和乌稔果的颜色相同，而且香味四溢，雷万兴很高兴，畲族人民为了纪念雷万兴的英雄事迹，也在每年的三月三出门他请，采集乌稔叶，做乌饭。

除了与畲族英雄雷万兴有关以外，还有另外一个关于乌饭的传说，

很久很久以前的一年三月，由于年前受山蚂蚁虫害，收成不好，再加上山主加租增税，畲山一开春，家家户户断了炊烟，可恶的山主连谷种也抢走。人断粮，挖野菜抗

饥，地断种，来年日子怎么过？畲家人的苦歌唱得多凄凉：

三月三，苦时光，畲家户户无食粮，

田园无种难下犁，山主逼债似虎狼。

男人讨食死路上，女人外出当奶娘。

撇下老母与幼儿，长哭短号好凄凉。

可是，狼心狗肺的山主却幸灾乐祸，他们不但不借出谷种，反而放凶狠的狗，把前来求借的畲人咬得鲜血淋淋。

实在忍耐不下去了，一天夜里，气壮如牛的蓝天风带了几个年轻力壮的后生仔翻墙进了山主大院，他们撬开粮仓的门，把黄澄的各种粮食一袋一袋地扛回畲山，连夜撒下田去。

How can they live? The songs sang by She people was miserable:

Households of She people had no grains, and their days were miserable on March 3rd.

They had no seeds to plough in fields, and the mountain masters pressed for debts like a tiger and wolf.

Men died on the road when they begged for food, and women went out to be wet nurses.

They left their old parents and young children, and cries were so miserable.

However, the brutal mountain masters took pleasure in other people's misfortunes, and they didn't lend grain seeds, but let out fierce dogs to bite She people who came to borrow seeds.

One night, strong Lan Tianfeng led several young men to turn over the walls of the mountain maters because they couldn't restrain their rage, and they opened the doors of the barns, carried bags of seed to She Mountain, and threw them to the fields.

The mountain masters found the barns were stolen, then they led a dozen of hatchet men to She Mountain like mad dogs on the next day. In order to prevent his villagers from suffering disaster, Lan Tianfeng stood up. However, he was locked in the dungeon by the mountain masters on February 3rd.

Lan Tianfeng was covered with wounds in the dungeon, the mountain masters conspired with Wry Mouth guarding the dungeon, and they didn't give rice to him and wanted to starve him to death.

After the information spread, She people came to visit him, and they pounded the remaining millet into rice, and boiled it and made it to rice balls. However, the rice balls were eaten by Wry Mouth, while Lan Tianfeng, who was the good young fellow of She people, ate nothing.

One day, Zhong Xiu, the most excellent singer of She Mountain, went to the dungeon to send food. This clever young woman thought a good way to punish Wry Mouth.

At noon, Zhong Xiu held the bamboo basket, there was a burlap bag in it, and she came to send food.

第二天，山主发现粮仓被盗，就带了十几个打手，疯犬似地扑向畲山。蓝天风为了使乡亲们免遭毒手，挺身站了出来。他被山主关进了地牢，这天刚好是二月初三。

在地牢里，蓝天风被打得浑身是伤，山主还串通看牢的歪嘴，不给蓝天风饭吃，想让他活活饿死。

消息传出，畲家父老姐妹们纷纷前去探监，他们用撒田剩下的谷子春成米，煮成饭并捏成饭团送进地牢。可饭团却落进歪嘴的肚里，畲家的好后生蓝天风还是未能吃到一粒饭。

这天，去池牢送饭的是畲山最出色的歌手钟秀姑娘。这个聪明的姑娘想出了一个治歪嘴的好办法。

时近晌午，钟秀挎着竹篓，竹篓里装着麻布袋，送饭来了。

歪嘴一边用下流的目光盯着姑娘，一边打开麻布袋的口子把手伸进去。这时，歪嘴突然鬼声怪调地乱喊起来，接着就手脚乱蹦乱舞起来。可是竹篓口子小，舞了半天还是舞不出来，疼得歪嘴满地打滚。原来，麻布袋里装的是又黑又大又毒的山蚂蚁。歪嘴被毒蚁一咬，当天夜里就发高热，讲胡话，天没亮就一命呜呼了。

从此以后，畬家人就从山上采来乌饭叶柴煮乌饭，煮出的乌米饭远远看去好像抱成一团的山蚂蚁，那些被山蚁吓破狗胆的狱卒们再也不敢吃饭团了！而且乌米饭极像山蚁，吃了它如同吃了山蚁，来年就不受蚁害了。

一年过去了，两年又过去了，蓝天风天天吃这乌米饭，不但伤口愈合，还添了不少气力。因此在畬山，乌米饭还有治乏力祛百病一说。

Staring at the young woman indecently, Wry Mouth opened the burlap bag and put his hand into it. At his moment, Wry Mouth cried strangely, and jumped around. However, the bamboo basket was too small, he couldn't take out his hand, and he lashed around in great pain. There were big black poisonous mountain ants in the burlap bag. Wry Mouth was bitten by the poisonous ants. He raved in a fever at that night, and died before the dawn.

Hereafter, She people came to mountain to pluck black rice leaves to boil black rice, which looked like mountain ants held together in a group and the jailers who were scared by mountain ants dared not to eat rice balls! The black rice looked like mountain ants, eating it liked eating mountain ants, which symbolizes people will not suffer from ant pest in the coming year.

One year passed, two years passed, Lan Tianfeng ate the black rice everyday, his wounds were healed, and his strength was added. Therefore, it's said that black rice can cure lacking in strength and get rid of a hundred of diseases.

On March 3rd of the third year, Lan Tianfeng was saved by his brothers in the uprising and was elected as the leader of the insurgent group. In order to let the later generations remember the uneasy rice of She people, "March 3rd" was fixed as the birthday of rice.

White rice turn into bright black rice, which looks like wearing clothes. Therefore, She Mountain people boil black rice in order to put clothes on rice ,which means to let it have a birthday. It's said that She people like to wear dark blue gunny clothes because they realize a reason from making black rice. Wearing this kind of clothes can prevent people from sunlight or biting of ants[1].

She people hold the song fair on this day, they get together to sing songs and dance lively.

到了第三年三月三这天，蓝天风终于被起义造反的兄弟救了出来，并推选为义军首领。为了让子孙后代记住畲家的米饭来之不易，"三月三"就订为谷米的生日。

谷米从白花花变成了乌亮亮，真像穿上衣裳似的，因此，畲山还有煮乌米饭是为了给谷米穿衣裳，好让它过生日之意。据传，畲家人通常喜欢穿的深蓝色麻布衣就是从这儿悟出的道理。穿上这种衣裳，不但可以防日头毒晒，而且山蚂蚁也不敢来咬叮呢[1]。

畲族人民还在这一天举行歌会，聚集在一起盘歌、跳舞，别提多热闹了。

[1]Collection of Chinese Folk Customs and Sources (Volume of Holidays and Seasons), pp169–171.

[1]雪犁 等主编，《中华民俗源流集成（节日岁时卷）》，甘肃人民出版社，1994年，第169–171页

在青海的土族地区，每年农历的三月初三是传统的鸡蛋会。在这一天里，除了要去寺庙里烧香献牲、请法师念经酬神之外，还要将鸡蛋煮熟，随身携带，在祭祀仪式结束后食用鸡蛋，以禳灾祛祸，保五谷丰登，人畜兴旺。而云南红河的哈尼族，则在这一天里做糯米粑粑和腌鸭蛋吃，这还有一个故事呢。

Tu people of Qinghai hold the traditional egg fair on lunar March 3rd each year. On this day, people go to temples to burn incenses, sacrifice animals, ask masters to chant sutras to reward gods, as well as boil eggs, bring them and eat them after the completion of the sacrifice ceremony in order to get rid of disasters and avoid misfortunes, bless a bumper harvest and prosperity of people and animal. Hani people in Red River of Yunnan make glutinous rice cakes and salted duck eggs, and there is a related story.

It was said that grass turned green in spring, the shepherd boy Suola came to play the reed pipe. Suola rode the ox, climbed mountains and ridges. The places over which the melodious whistling played by Suola flew had green mountain and water, leaves grew out and flowers bloomed. Hani people laughed, began to plough and sow in spring, and transplanted rice seedlings in terraced fields.

Unfortunately, the ox of the shepherd boy Suola stumbled and fell from the rock and Suola dropped to his death. His blood dyed peach flowers red, his sweat dyed pear flowers white, and his tears dyed grass green. Since then, grass and trees turned green automatically, the peach flowers became pink,

传说古时候，春季到了，草要发绿，得要天边来的牧童索腊来吹牧笛。索腊年年骑着牛，走过一座又一座山，翻过一座又一座岭。凡是索腊悠扬的笛声飞到的地方，山也青了，水也绿了，叶也发了，花也开了。哈尼人笑开了，便开始春耕播种，把秧苗插满遍岭的梯田。

不幸，有一年，牧童索腊的牛失蹄从岩石上摔下去，索腊被摔死了。他的血染红了桃花，他的汗染白了梨花，眼泪浇绿了青草。从那时候起，每年春天，草木才会自动发绿，桃花才成了粉红的花

朵，就像索腊的脸蛋，梨花才成了洁白的花朵，就像索腊纯洁的心灵①。

据说为了纪念索腊，每年夏历的三月初三，孩子们就穿上节日盛装，带上糯米粑粑、腌鸭蛋、腊肉到山上去游玩，这也被称为哈尼族的儿童节。孩子们还要给索腊留一个位置，请他来和大家一起吃饭。而且，在这一天，牛都要关在圈里作为惩罚，鸡鸭鹅都要关在笼子里以避讳。

which looked like the face of Suola, and the pear flower turned white, which were like the pure heart of Suola[1].

In order to commemorate Suola, children wear festival attires, bring glutinous rice cakes, salted duck eggs and cured meat and come to mountains to play on March 3rd of the Xia Calendar every year, which is called the Children's Day of Hani people. Children leave a place for Suola and invite him to have meal with them. Moreover, oxen are detained in pen as a punishment, chicken, ducks and gooses are detained in cages in order to avoid taboo.

①雪犁等主编，《中华民俗源流集成（节日岁时卷）》，甘肃人民出版社，1994年，第157页

[1]Collection of Chinese Folk Customs and Sources (Volume of Holidays and Seasons), p157.

4 载 歌 载 舞
Singing and Dancing

Singing songs and dancing are necessary in the celebration activity, especially in minority areas. Minorities such as Buyi people, Zhuang people and Dong people etc. who have talent and tradition of singing song and dancing hold national dances to celebrate on March 3rd. March 3rd of Buyi people in Guiyang is called "cutworm fair" as well as "sacrificing cutworm". It was said that people found cutworm climbed out to bite shoots after sowing in spring. People thought that cutworm was the heavenly horse, and they shall feed "heavenly horses" with fried corns after the spring sowing in order to prevent shoots from being bitten. Hereafter, Buyi people bring fired corns to slopes to pray for favorable climatic weather and a bumper harvest on March 3rd. Buyi people in the north of Guizhou climb mountains for spring outing on March 3rd,

唱歌跳舞，是庆祝活动中必不可少的一个环节，尤其是少数民族地区，颇具歌舞天赋和传统的布依族、壮族、侗族等等少数民族同胞在三月初三的时候跳起民族舞蹈庆祝。贵阳的布依族的三月三俗称"地蚕会"，又叫做"祭地蚕"。据说在古代，人们发现春天播种之后有地蚕爬出来咬死禾苗。当时的人们认为地蚕是天上的天马，要在春播之后炒包谷粒来喂"天马"，才能避免禾苗被咬。从此以后，布依族人民就在三月三的时候炒包谷粒带到山坡上祈求风调雨顺，禾稻丰收。黔北的布依族在三月三的时候到山上去踏青，把糯米饭染成五颜六色，作为礼物赠送给亲戚朋友。青年男女们在山坡上吹木叶，唱山歌。

还有一些地区的布依族同胞将三月三称为"赶毛杉树"，又叫"毛杉树歌节"，为期三天，男女老少都到河边听青年们对歌、盘歌。歌手们凭借吟唱的天赋，大显身手，吸引不少女孩的目光。关于这一节日，也有一个传说。

and they dye glutinous rice colorful and send it to relatives and friends as a present. Young women and men go to slopes to cut tree leaves and sing mountain songs.

Buyi people in some areas call March 3rd "Going to Firs" as well as "Fir Song Festival", which lasts three days, all people come to riverside to listen to songs in antiphonal style sang by young people. Singers show their talent of singing and attract attention of girls. There is a legend about the festival.

Ashan and Ashu, the couple were hardworking and grew crops like all the villagers and lived a happy life. Ashu often sang songs when she worked, her singing voice was fair, it flew over Pan River and mountains, even sparrows kept silence, colorful clouds in the sky didn't want to move. Lotus Song Fairy was startled by the singing voice of Ashu, she rode a five-colored cloud, flew in the air to listen to the songs for nine days, and didn't want to leave.

Because Lotus Song Fairy loved the singing voice of Ashu, she rode a five-colored cloud and appeared in the dream of Ashu, "Many locusts will come to your villages in a few days, and they will eat up all crops in the villages. However, these locusts fear golden voice, you sing well, but you don't have a golden voice, and they aren't afraid of your voice. Now I give the golden voice to you, the locusts will not destroy crops any more if they hear your golden voice. They will fly to Cloud Nine to be the food of my cat after hearing your voice." After saying the words, Lotus Song Fairy touched her throat, and then touched Ashu's throat for three times, then rode on the five-colored cloud and flew

阿杉和阿树夫妻两个和四乡八寨的人们一样，勤快种庄稼，过着好日子。阿树总是一边干活一边唱歌，歌声悠憨，飞过盘江，飞过山头，唱得阳雀不敢出声，唱得天上彩云不想溜走，阿树的歌声，惊动了九重天上的莲花歌仙，莲花歌仙就驾着一朵五色彩云，飘呀飘的飞到半天云里来听，一连听了九天还不想走。

一天半夜，莲花歌仙由于很喜欢阿树的歌声，就驾着一朵五色彩云来托梦给阿树说："过些日子，会有很多麻抓（蝗虫）来到你们这，要来刨光你们四乡寨所有的庄稼哩。不过，这些麻抓妖怪是最怕金嗓子，你的歌唱得很好，可惜不是金嗓子，麻抓不怕。现在我把金嗓子换给你，以后，只要一听到你的金嗓在唱歌，麻抓就不敢来糟蹋庄稼了，他们会随着你的歌声飘到九重天上来给我喂我的猫。"莲花歌仙说完，用手摸了摸自己的喉咙，然后又摸了摸阿树的喉咙，连摸了三遍以后就驾着五色彩云飞走了。阿树一觉醒来，只觉喉咙痒痒，就一连嚼了几节甘草，喉咙才不痒了，觉得很清爽。这天，阿树和阿杉在田里做活，阿树像往常一样唱起了歌，声音特别清脆婉转，听了真是饭不吃都饱，酒不渴自醉。

这年六月间，四乡八寨的庄稼长得青油油的，秧子正在打苞。一天，阿树和阿杉正在自家的田里薅草遣秧，一边祈祷一边唱歌来舒心解累。晌午时候，突然从西方飞来一群一群的麻抓，像一堵一堵的乌云一样，落在田坝里，"喊喊喳喳"地咬着秧苞。说来也奇怪，麻抓听到阿树的金嗓子歌声，就不敢落在她和阿杉在的这块地里。这时，阿树想起了梦中莲花歌仙的话，就对阿杉说"九重天上的莲花歌仙既然给了我一副金嗓子，要我唱歌来驱赶麻抓。现在麻抓这么多，我们不能只在自家田里

away. When Ashu woke up, she felt her throat itching, so she chewed liquorice and her throat wasn't itching and felt refreshing. Ashu and Ashan worked in the field, Ashu sang song as usual, her voice was melodious and fair, and people reveled in her voice.

Crops of villages grew green and seedling produced ears in June in this year. One day, Ashu and Ashan were getting rid of weeds and nursing seedlings, they prayed and sang songs to feel happy and refresh themselves. At noon, groups of locusts flew from the west like black clouds, and stopped in fields, and bit ears of seedlings. Strangely, the locusts didn't stop in the fields of Ashu and Ashan when they heard the golden voice of Ashu. At this moment, Ashu remembered the words of Lotus Song Fairy in her dream, she said to Ashan that, "Lotus Song Fairy on Cloud Nine gave me a golden voice, and let me sing songs stop the locusts. There are so many locusts, we shall not only sing in our fields, I shall sing my golden voice in all villages, and drive all the locusts to Cloud Nice to feed the golden cat of Lotus Song Fairy, so that all people can have a good harvest, food and clothes."

After hearing her words, Ashan said, "It's a good idea! You sing as soon as possible! I will accompany you to sing in all directions, and drive away all the locusts." In this way, Ashu sang in her golden voice from this field to that field, from this plain to that plain, from this village to that village, she sang songs for twenty-seven days without stop, arrived at Dewo, the voice drove the locusts out of sight, and they were driven to Cloud Nine to feed the golden cat of Lotus Song Fairy. Crops were saved, the villages had a bumper harvest, and people showed their gratitude to Ashu and Ashan.

However, Ashu had sang songs for twenty-seven days, she was sick because of fatigue, she didn't want to eat or drink, and didn't become better after having many herbal medicines. People worried about her, so they came to see her like long lines of going to market, and they hoped that she could recover quickly to sing songs to make people feel happy and be refreshed to drive away pests. Some

唱，要用这副金嗓子唱到四乡八寨去，把所有麻抓赶到九重天去给莲花歌仙喂她的金猫，让大家都得到好收成，人人有饭吃，个个有衣穿。"

阿杉听了，忙说："要得要得!你快唱吧!唱到四面八方去，我陪着你，把所有的麻抓通通赶走。"就这样，阿树亮开了金嗓子，从这块田唱到那块田，从这个田坝唱到那个田坝，从这个寨子唱到那个寨子，一连唱了三九二十七天没有歇气，一直唱到了德卧地方，歌声把麻抓赶得无影无踪，都赶上了九重天给莲花歌仙喂金猫去了。庄稼保住了，村村寨寨又得到了好收成，人人感谢阿树和阿杉。

可是，阿树一直唱了二十七天歌，过于劳累，就病倒了，饭不思，水不想，吃了几多草药都不见好，人人替她着急，个个为她担心。来看望她的人很多，像赶场一样排成长线，都祝愿她快快康复，好为大家唱歌舒心解闷，驱赶害虫。有的边递芭蕉边对她说："你是我们布依族的歌仙呀，只要一天听不到你的歌声，就懒心无肠的，活路都少做几多，饭也少吃几口呢。"

可是，阿树的病总不见好，水不沾，饭不挨，第二年古历三月初三赶场那天，她终于离开了人世！噩耗传出，山也低头，河水在哭，芭蕉叶在流泪，楠竹弯了腰。人们更是难过，人人悲伤，个个痛哭。大家再也听不到布依族歌仙阿树的金嗓歌声了。这天，人们含着眼泪，把阿树安埋在者棉寨和纳拿寨之间的一个土包上。

再说阿杉，由于他一直陪着阿树到四乡八寨去唱歌驱赶麻抓，已够累了，又加上日夜守护在阿树的身边，更是劳累，吃不下，睡不着，身体都熬瘦了。如今，阿树一死，他更是悲伤，哭得死去活来，第二天，他也离开了

people passed banana to her and said to her, "You are the song fairy of our Buyi people. We are in bad mood without your singing voice, and we work and eat less."

However, the disease of Ashu cannot be cured, she didn't drink or eat and died on lunar March 3rd, the day of going to market. The bad news broke, the mountains lowered their heads, the rivers cried, the banana leaves shed tears and the bamboos bent down. People felt sorry and sad, and they cried painfully. They cannot hear the golden voice of Ashu, the song fairy of Buyi people. On this day, people buried Ashu on a mound between Zhemian Village and Nana Village in tears.

Ashan accompanied Ashu, who sang songs to drive the locusts in the villages, he was so tired and guarded Ashu days and nights, he became thinner because he couldn't eat and sleep. When Ashu died, he became sadder, wept his heart out, and left the world on the next day. People buried him with Ashu on the mound in tears.

Soon after Ashu and Ashan were buried, two firs grew in front of their tombs. People said that these two firs were the embodiment of Ashu and Ashan. Strangely, these two firs grew in winds, they grew high and large soon, their leaves were thin and long and overhanged like the hair of Ashu. In order to commemorate the couple Ashu and Ashan, they were called Raw Firs. The mound on which they were buried was also called the place of Raw Firs. Afterwards, young women and men in the villages wore festival attires, they came to the place of Raw Fires in groups, they blew leaves and played different musical instruments, including sibling flutes, Jew's harps, *lusheng* and *yueqin* on the first day of going to market since March 3rd, so that they can commemorate Ashu and Ashan to learn their honorable virtues as well as looking for lovers in songs and whistling, they also admired the everlasting love between Ashan and Ashu. They came to ask for the golden voice from Ashu, which was the golden voice of Buyi people, so that they can use singing voice to drive all pests and protect crops when they transplanted and nursed seedlings, and they can have a good harvest in autumn. With

人世。人们含着眼泪，也把他安葬在小土包上和阿树在一起。

　　阿树和阿杉安葬不久，他们的坟前就长出了两棵杉树，个个都说，这两棵杉树就是阿杉和阿树的化身哩！说也奇怪，这两棵杉树能见风长，不久就长得又高又大，枝叶又细又长，往下倒垂着，真像阿树在生时披着的头发一样。人们为了纪念阿树和阿杉两夫妻，就把这两棵杉树取名叫"毛杉树"。他们埋葬的这个小土包，也就叫做毛杉树地名了。从那以后，每年三月三第一个赶场天，四乡八寨的男女青年，都穿着节日的盛装，邀邀约约，成群结队，有的吹木叶，有的吹姊妹箫，有的吹口弦，有的吹芦笙，有的弹月琴，来到毛杉树地方，一面纪念阿树和阿杉，学他们高尚的品德；一面唱歌吹哨找情侣，要像阿杉和阿树一样永远相爱。更主要的是来向布依族金歌嗓仙阿树讨金嗓子，以便在插秧和藓秧时，学着金嗓歌仙阿树用歌声把麻抓和一切害虫赶走，保护庄稼，秋来得到好收成。久而久之，三月三赶毛杉树就成了布依族和各族青年男女的传统歌仙节。

贵州安龙县的布依族同胞在三月三这一天除了去河边看青年们对歌，孩子们还比赛划竹排呢。父母给孩子们做好糯米饭和鸡蛋带到山坡上吃。另外还有一个传说，说三月三是山神的生日，为了避免山神生气危害人间，在这

the lapse of time, going to the firs on March 3rd has become the traditional song fairy festival of Buyi people and young men and women of minorities.

Buyi people of Anlong County in Guizhou go to riverside to watch young people singing in antiphonal style and children holding bamboo raft competition. Parents make glutinous rice and boil eggs for children, so that they can bring them to slopes to eat. According to another legend, March 3rd was the birthday of the Mountain God, people in the village came to the entrance to place the

altar and sacrificed to the Mountain God with the offerings such as rooster, dog blood, and paper flags etc. in order to prevent him from being angry and endangering the world. Then households invited witches to their houses to hold ceremonies of getting rid of evil spirits and devils, witches came back to the altar at the entrance and suppressed the evil spirits and devils in front of the holy spirits after the cleaning of the whole village was completed.

Dong people go to vegetable gardens to pluck onion and garlic and put them to a bamboo basket and pass it to an ideal young man on March 3rd. If two young people are interested in each other, they come to a slope to sing songs in antiphonal style, they look for bosom friends with songs, and they dance in the opening in the center of the village. A story about the blooming of the tung tree is popular among Baojing Dong people. It was said that the blooming of the tung tree was seen as the time to transplant seedlings, but the tung tree forgot to bloom one year, farming works were delayed, and people had to escape to the area of Baojing. In order to avoid the reoccurrence of the event, people played *lusheng* and sang songs on lunar March 3rd, reminded everyone of the time of transplanting seedlings for fear of delaying farming season. This day is also called "Firecracker Festival".

一天里全寨人民要一起到村寨口摆设神坛，用雄鸡、狗血、纸旗等供品祭祀山神。然后家家户户都要请巫师到自己家来做仪式，扫去邪灵恶鬼，整个村寨都打扫完毕后，巫师再回到寨口的神坛前将收来的妖魔鬼怪镇压在神灵之前。

贵州的侗族同胞在三月三时，要到菜园去摘采葱蒜，放在竹篮里，递给看中的男孩子。如果双方都有意思，就会到山坡边对歌，以歌声觅知音，还在寨子中心的空地上跳舞。在报京侗族同胞中流传了一个桐树开花的故事。据说古代的时候，大家都以桐树开花为插秧的时间，但是有一年，桐树忘了开花，耽误了农活，只好逃到报京一带。为了避免这种事情再次发生，人们每逢农历三月初三九吹芦笙唱歌，互相提醒插秧时间到了，免得误了农时。这一天也被称为"花炮节"。

　　瑶族同胞将三月三称为"干巴节"，在这一天里，人们集体渔猎，按户分配，再到广场上唱歌跳舞，谈情说爱。三月三也是海南黎族人民欢乐的日子，在这一天，男女青年盛装打扮，跳起竹排舞，唱着动人的山歌，欢庆佳节。说到三月三，还有一个代代相传的传说。

Yao people call March 3rd "Ganba Festival", they fish and hunt collectively and distribute things according to household, then they come to squares to sing songs and dance, and talk about love. March 3rd is also a happy day of Li people of Hainan, young men and women dress up, play bamboo dance, and sing fair mountain songs to celebrate the grand festival on this day. As for March 3rd, there is a legend which has been passed down for generations.

It was said that rivers flooded plains and ridges and overwhelmed everything on the earth in the ancient times, only a brother and a sister left, who were Tianfei and Guanyin . They held a gourd, and floated in the surging flood, when they floated to Yanwo Ridge beside Changhua River, they were stuck on the branch of a big lattice tree. After a while, the flood vanished gradually, and the two siblings lived at last. However, there was deathly silence on the earth, they lived lonely. Therefore, the two siblings decided to look for relatives separately. When departing from each other, they decided to meet again on Yanwo Ridge on March 3rd every year. They traveled all over the world, but they couldn't find anyone. The brother cannot find a woman to marry, and the younger sister cannot find a man to marry. After many years, the siblings became old, and human beings faced the danger of extinction. The sister made her decision. She made tattoos on her face, so the brother couldn't recognize his sister. The siblings married on Yanwo Ridge and bore children.

相传远古时候，洪水泛滥，淹没了平原和山岭，吞没了大地的一切，只剩兄妹两人——天妃和观音，他们抱住了葫芦飘，在滔滔的洪水中到处漂泊，漂啊漂啊，他们漂流到昌化江畔的燕窝岭，被一棵大格树的树丫卡住了。过了些时候，洪水慢慢消退了，兄妹俩总算活了下来。可是，大地上死一样静寂，只剩他俩孤零零地生活着。因此，兄妹俩决定分头去寻找亲人。临走前，两人约定每年三月三回到燕窝岭相会。他们走遍了天涯海角，到处都见不到人迹。哥哥找不到女郎配偶，妹妹找不到男子成亲。年长月久，眼见兄妹两人快要衰老，人类就要灭种了。妹妹暗地里拿定主意，在自己脸上刺上了花纹，这一来，哥哥认不出纹脸的妹妹。于是，在这一年的三月三，兄妹俩就在燕窝岭结为夫妻，生男育女。

婚后，他们朝出暮归，勤耕勤作，在河畔挖水塘养鱼，在燕窝岭种植木棉、芒果和山棟树，还在半山腰开凿一个石洞居住。洞的上面是悬崖陡壁，野兽不敢来犯，洞的下面峭壁万丈，山洪水涨也淹不到。每午三月三日，正是山花烂漫，红棉争艳，山棟飘香的时候，观音和天妃便率领着子孙们一起载歌载舞，迎接春天的到来。后来不知过了多久，天妃和观音便死在山洞里，化成了观音石。黎家子孙后代为纪念天妃和观音，也就把石洞取名为娘母洞。每逢三月三日，男女老少都要携带桶米做的糕点、粽子，从四面八方赶到这里来。他们拿弓箭、鱼叉在溪里捉鱼，在溪边煮饭，把鱼用火烤熟，与粽子、糕点一起放在洞口祭拜。

After the marriage, they went out early and returned late every day, worked hard to produce crops, dug pools beside rivers for fish farming, planted silk cotton, mango and aphanamixis, and they dug a cave on the halfway of the mountain. There were steep and perilous cliff above the cave, so beasts couldn't attack them, there were also deep precipices below the cave, and torrential floods couldn't drown it. On March 3rd, it's the time of blooming mountain flowers, silk cotton and fragrant aphanamixis, Guanyin and Tianfei led their generations to sing songs and dance to meet the coming of spring. After a long time, Tianfei and Guanyin died in the cave and turned into Guanyin stones. Li generations called the cave Mother Cave. On March 3rd, all people bring cakes and *zongzi* made of glutinous rice and come here from all directions. They hold bow, arrow and fork to catch fishes in streams, boil rice beside streams, roast fishes, and place *zongzi* and cakes in front of the cave for worship.

Zhuang people of Guangxi also make five-colored glutinous rice on March 3rd, erect maple leaves on doors, and sing Zhuang songs around cloth sheds. As for the reason why people go to song fair on this day, there is an impressive local legend:

It was said that there was a Zhuang person whose name was Wei Dagui, and he was a courtier of a local tyrant. Dagui was young, but he had great learning and outstanding talent. He concerned about sufferings of Zhuang people, and brought most of his salary endowed by the local emperor to his hometown to help the poor and save the hungry, he was honest and remained poor all the time. One year, Zhuang Village had a great drought, the villagers begged Dagui to present a memorial to the local tyrant for exemption from imperial grain, and Dagui knelt and said, "Zhuang Village had no harvest, and I will accompany you to investigate the condition." Dagui accompanied the tyrant to Zhuang Village, and they saw dry fields, scorched spikes, and groups of common people with lean and hunger looking who knelt on the mountain roads to complain. Dagui knelt and said, "Your majesty! You see everything, and I hope that you can exempt them from imperial grains." The local tyrant had no choice and had to exempt Zhuang Village from imperial grains. Since then, he hated Dagui very much, but he couldn't

广西的壮族在三月初三这一天也要制作五色糯米饭，在门上插上枫树叶，男女老少围着布棚唱壮歌。

为什么要在这一天赶歌圩，当地也有一个感人的传说。

相传，在很久以前，壮乡有个姓韦名叫达桂的人，在一个土皇帝手下当臣相。达桂年纪不大，但学识渊博，才能过人，而且十分关心壮家百姓的疾苦，土皇赐给他俸禄，他将一大半拿回家乡济贫救饥，自己却两袖清风，一无所有。有一年，壮乡大旱，乡亲们求达桂向土皇帝奏免王粮，达桂跪奏道："壮乡百姓颗粒无收，吾伴千岁前往视察。"达桂伴驾来到壮乡，只见田土龟裂，禾穗枯焦，一群群面黄肌瘦的百姓跪在山道上告苦。达桂也下跪道："千岁亲见，万望免粮。"土皇帝无奈，只好免去壮乡王粮。打那以后，他对达桂恨之入骨，可是鉴于达桂的声望，又找不出什么岔子把他除掉，因此施出毒计，阴谋陷害达桂。

一天，土皇把达桂唤到跟前，说："达桂，你向来很能干，现在想叫你给我办一件好事。"达桂一听，就知道土皇不怀好意，但他却从容地说，"请千岁道来，小人哪有不从之理。"土皇帝半眯着眼睛说："我正在建造一座楼阁，缺少瓦片，听说壮人的皮能防寒防暑，防水防火，经久耐用，你要在两个月内给我弄九百张壮人皮来当瓦片用，到时重重有赏，如过期误了大事要从严惩罚。"达杜轻松地应道："到时，请千岁亲自跟车辆到城门下点货拉收。"

一个月过去，达桂没有动静，五十九天过去了，达桂依然没有一点动静。限期到了，达桂才召集九百个壮家大汉，每人带一斤糯米、一斤米酒、一斤辣椒粉，来

find a way to get rid of him due to his reputation, so he thought over a venomous scheme to frame up Dagui.

One day, the local tyrant called Dagui and said, "Dagui, you have been competent, and I want to ask you to do a good thing for me now." After hearing his words, Dagui knew that he was harboring an evil scheme, but he answered calmly, "Please tell me, and I will obey you of course." The local tyrant said with half-closed eyelids, "I am building a pavilion, but tiles are lacked, I hear that skin of Zhuang people can prevent coldness, heatstroke, water and fire, you shall get nine hundred pieces of human skins for me as tiles within two months, I will reward you greatly if you make it on time, and I will punish you strictly if you delay the event." Dagui answered easily, "Please come to the gate of the city to receive them by yourself on time."

One month passed, Dagui did nothing; fifty-nine days passed, Dagui did nothing. The term expired, Dagui convened nine hundred Zhuang men, each man brought one *jin* of glutinous rice, one *jin* of pepper powder, came to the imperial city, they set up pots to steam glutinous rice and boil pepper vegetable soup, they took off their coats, stripped to the waist, sat under the city gate and drank liquor, had pepper soup and ate glutinous rice. When they ate and drank to repletion, and were reeking with sweat, the local tyrant who sat in a large sedan chair and was carried by eight people came. Dagui came up and bowed, "I have sent the goods to your majesty, but these Zhuang men were miserable wretches, their skins leaked water. Do you still want them? " The local tyrant came out of the sedan and came up to have a look. Their black and red skins were wet as if they were taken out from water, and an offensive smell greeted him. The local tyrant covered his nose, wrinkled his brows, stepped back and said, "They are slack, stinking and useless!" After saying the words, he turned back his sedan and returned to his palace.

When one plot failed, he tried another. When Tomb-Sweeping Day approached, the local tyrant called Dagui, and pretended to be honest and said, "Dagui, you have been clever. I have one thing that shall be done by you!" Hearing his words, Dagui knew that the local tyrant was malicious, but he said without fear, "Please tell me! I will obey you." The local tyrant said with half-closed eyelids, "I need a pig head which is as heavy as the mountain behind the palace for ancestor sacrifice on Tomb-Sweeping

到皇城脚下，架锅蒸糯米饭，煮辣椒菜汤，一个个脱掉上衣，光着膀子，坐在城门下饮酒，喝辣椒汤，吃糯米饭。正当个个酒足饭饱，满身汗水淋漓的时候，土皇帝坐着八抬大轿赶到了。达桂连忙上前施了个礼道："货物已给千岁送来，可是这帮壮佬贱骨头，张张皮都是漏水的，能用得着吗？"土皇帝下轿上前一看，一个个黑里透红的皮肤上湿漉漉的，像是刚从水里捞起来似的，一股臭气扑鼻。土皇帝用手捂着鼻子，皱着眉头，后退几步说："又漏水又臭，不能用，不能用！"说完，调转轿头回宫殿去了。

一计未成，又生二计。快到清明节，土皇帝又把达桂唤到跟前，装着十分诚恳的模样说："达桂，你向来很聪明，现在我有一件事非得要你去办不行。"达桂一听，就知道土皇帝又怀恶意，但却毫无畏惧地说道："请说来，鄙人哪有抗拒之理。"土皇帝眯着眼睛说；"清明节我需要一个像宫殿后面那座大山一样重的猪头来祭祖，你给我在一个月内弄来，到时重重有赏，过期误了大事要从严惩罚！"达桂十分轻松地笑着说："好办，好办。"

二十天过去了，达桂没有动静。三十天过去了，达桂依然没有一点动静。限期过了，土皇帝派兵来抓达桂，达桂扛着一杆大秤和兵差一道去见土皇帝："皇上大人，壮家比山头一样大的猪多得很，就不知道宫殿后面那座大山究竟有多重，请皇上用这杆秤去称一称，我回去好照称猪头叫人抬来。""噢?……这……"土皇帝哑口无言，达桂又战胜了土皇帝。

土皇帝见达桂的确聪
留在宫殿里是
非除掉不可，
更恶劣的
又把

Day, you need to bring it to me within one month, I will reward you greatly if you make it on time, and I will punish you strictly if you delay the event!" Dagui said light-heartedly, "It's easy! It's easy!"

Twenty days passed, Dagui did nothing. Thirty days passed, he still did nothing. The term expired, the local tyrant assigned his army to grasp Dagui. Dagui carried a large scale to see the local tyrant with the soldiers, "Your majesty, Zhuang people have many pigs which are bigger than the mountain, but I don't know the weight of the mountain behind the palace, could you use the scale to weigh it, then I could come back to weigh the pig head and ask people to carry it here." "Oh?...It…" The local tyrant was dumbfounded, and Dagui defeated the local tyrant again.

The local tyrant saw cleverness of Dagui, and thought that he was a curse in the palace, and he must be eliminated, so the tyrant thought over a more malicious scheme. One day, he called Dagui to him and said, "Dagui, you have been clever. The queen will be in the confinement in her childbirth after one month. It's said that eggs laid by cocks are very nutritious, you shall bring four hundred and ninety eggs laid by cocks within twenty days, I will reward you greatly if you make it on time, and I will punish you strictly if you delay the event." Dagui promised nicely, "I will send them to the queen by myself."

Ten days passed, Dagui did nothing; and twenty days passed, he still did nothing. The term expired, the local tyrant sent his army to grasp Dagui. Dagui came up and bowed, he said to the soldiers apologetically, "I'm terribly sorry. My father delivered a boy when I returned home, he was in the confinement in his childbirth, and I have to take care of him for forty-nine days according to the rules of our Zhuang people. You go back and tell the queen, I will send her the eggs of cocks when the confinement is over." The soldiers said loudly, "How does a man deliver a child?" Dagui smiled and said, "A man cannot deliver a child. How can a cock lay eggs?" The soldiers could say nothing more, they had to return and told it to the local tyrant. The tyrant was very angry, and he ordered the soldiers to capture Dagui and bring him to justice.

"达桂，你向来聪明能干，再过一个月皇后就要坐月子了，听说壮家的公鸡蛋很有营养，你给我在二十天内弄四百九十个公鸡蛋，到时重重有赏，过期要从严惩罚！"达桂满口答应道："到时，我亲自给皇后送来。"

十天过去了，达桂没有动静，二十天过去了，达桂依然没有一点动静。限期过了，土皇帝派兵来抓达桂，达桂连忙上前施礼，装着十分歉意的样子对兵差说："非常对不起，我刚回家那天，父亲就生下了一个男孩，现在正在坐月子，按照我们壮家的规矩，我得照料七七四十九天才行，请你们回禀皇上，满四十九天以后，我再给皇上送去公鸡蛋。"兵差大声喝道："天下男子哪有生小孩的？"达桂笑嘻嘻地答道："男人不生小孩，公鸡怎么生蛋呢？"兵差无话可说，只好回去禀告土皇，土皇得知，勃然大怒，立即下令捉拿达桂归案。

壮家乡亲闻讯连夜送达桂到山上的枫树林里躲起来。皇兵上山搜索，重重包围，只在山林里发现吃剩的糯米饭，就是找不到人。他们搜呀搜，一连搜了七天七夜，不见踪影，土皇无奈，就下令放火烧山，那一天正是夏历三月初三。皇兵走后，乡亲们进山找呀找，最后在山林里一棵合抱不过来的枫树洞里找到了达桂的尸体，大家含着眼泪把他葬在那棵大枫树旁，男女老少在墓前放声痛哭起来。哭呀！哭呀！泪水如同串串珍珠洒在坟上，坟上顿时长出了一棵棵嫩绿的小枫树，一丛丛翠蓝的红兰草和一株株翠绿的黄杞子树。为了纪念达桂，乡亲们又在墓旁建造了庙宇，名曰"达杜堂"。一个秀习还在庙堂里题了一首诗，至今这首诗还在壮乡流传。诗云：

壮家良才韦达桂，与皇智斗显神威。

When Zhuang villagers heard the information, they sent Dagui to the maple forest on the mountain to hide. The imperial soldiers climbed the mountain to look for him, besieged it heavily, but they only found the remaining glutinous rice, they couldn't find anyone. They searched for seven days and nights continuously, but they couldn't find the trace. The local tyrant had no way, so he ordered to burn the mountain, and it was March 3rd of the Xia calendar. After the imperial soldiers left, the villagers came into the mountain to look for him, and found his body in a cave of a large maple in the forest at last, they buried him beside the large maple in tears, many small green maples, blue orchids and green engelhardtia chrysolepis grew up on the tomb at once. In order to commemorate Dagui, the villagers built a temple beside his tomb, which was called as "Dagui Hall". A scholar wrote a poem in the temple hall, which has been spread among Zhuang village now. The poem wrote:

The talent of Zhuang people Wei Dagui had an encounter of wits with the tyrant,

He died on March 3rd, and left a good name for long ages.

Because Dagui liked to drink wine and eat glutinous rice and conquered the local tyrant in the ways of drinking wine and eating glutinous rice, and he was framed since he couldn't offer eggs of cocks, households of Zhuang took rice wine, glutinous rice and boiled eggs to the tomb of Dagui to memorize him On March 3rd of the next year,. When people were in great sorrow, there were the rumbling of thunder, flashing lightening, fierce gale and heavy rain in the sky, many maple leaves, red orchids and engelhardtia chrysolepis fell on bowls and plates, raindrops made the glutinous rice red, yellow, blue, purple and white and made eggs red and blue. When the storm stopped, a fire snake in five colors including red, yellow, blue, purple and white rushed out of the temple hall, and the big snake nodded its head for five times towards the villagers, and went straight to the palace and bit the local tyrant to death. Since then, Zhuang people in the west of Guangxi set up cloth sheds in villages on March 3rd of the Xia calendar every year in order to commemorate Dagui, because it's said that ghosts who died outside home cannot enter their houses, so they place the offerings including five-colored glutinous rice under the cloth sheds to sacrifice to the soul of Dagui, they sing praise songs around

三月初三殉躯体，百世流芳千古垂。

因为达桂生前喜欢喝酒、吃糯米饭，用喝酒、吃糯米饭的方式战胜了土皇帝，后又因拿不出公鸡蛋被陷害。所以到了第二年三月初三这一天，壮乡家家户户都拿着米酒、糯米饭和熟鸡蛋到达桂墓前祭奠。正当人们沉入哀思时，天空突然雷声隆隆，电光闪闪，狂风大作，大雨倾盆而巳在这凤吼雷鸣之中，只见一片片枫树叶、一丛丛红兰草、一颗颗黄杞子落在碗碟上，雨点打在上面，糯米饭呈现出红、黄、蓝、菁、白五种颜色，鸡蛋也呈现出红、蓝等几种颜色。雷雨一停，从庙堂里冲出一条身上呈现红、黄、蓝、紫、白五种颜色的火蛇，这条大蛇向乡亲们点了五次头后，就直奔宫殿把土皇帝咬死。从那时候起，桂西一带的壮族人家为了纪念达桂，年年到夏历三月初三这天，村村寨寨都搭起布棚，因为传说在外丧生的魂魄不进家，因此人们只好在布棚下摆上五色糯米饭等供品祭奠达桂的亡灵，在布棚周围唱起赞美和感谢达桂的赞歌。一代传一代，就形成了现在赶三月三歌圩的习俗①。

the cloth sheds to show gratitude to the dignity. The convention of going to song fair on March 3rd has been formed for generations[1].

①雪犁等主编，《中华民俗源流集成（节日岁时卷）》，甘肃人民出版社，1994年，第137—140页

[1]Collection of Chinese Folk Customs and Sources (Volume of Holidays and Seasons), pp137-140.

第四章

特色节庆地

三月三，真热闹，牛成群，马嘶叫，雪白羊儿满山跑。

三锐响，吓一跳，烧拜香的声调高。

木皮影，狗狗叫，猴翻筋斗蹦蹦跳。

西洋镜前人不少，打洋鼓，吹洋号，爷爷看了哈哈笑。

——陕西汉阴童谣

虽然三月三"上巳节"已经逐渐消失，但是众多习俗依然在清明节期间被实践。而且，少数民族的三月三，过得更加隆重、热烈，有庙会、对歌、舞蹈表演，还有各种各样风味独特的小吃吸引四面八方的游客。唱起来吧，跳起来吧，一起庆祝春光明媚的三月三！

Chapter Four

Places of Characteristic Celebration

It's lively on March 3rd, crowds of cattle are hustled, horses whinny and white sheep run all over mountains.

The sounds of cymbals scare people and the tones of people who burn incense are loud.

There are wooden shadow puppets, barking dogs and monkeys turning somersaults and jumping.

Many people stand in front of peep show, foreign drums are struck, foreign trumpets are played, and grandfathers laugh loudly.

——Children Ballad of Hanyin, Shaanxi

Although "Shangsi Festival" on March 3rd disappeared gradually, many conventions are still practiced during Tomb-Sweeping Festival. Moreover, March 3rd of minorities is celebrated more grandly and enthusiastically, temple fair, singing in antiphonal style, dance performance and various kinds of special snacks attract tourists from all directions. Let's sing and jump, and celebrate March 3rd in fine spring!

1

江都"三月三"庙会
March 3rd Temple Fair in Jiangdu

A large number of people from ancient towns of Jiangdu crowd to temples, streets and lanes on lunar March 3rd, and they soak in the happy atmosphere of the festival on the scene. According to the local tradition, March 3rd is the traditional festival of Fairy Temple. Fairy Temple in Jiangdu before the Han and Jin Dynasties was called "Longchuan", it was said that there was an immortal white dragon in this river, and it was also called "White Dragon River". It was said that a fairy showed the ways to Wu Zixu of the Warring States, Wu Zixu who achieved success and won recognition built a temple to worship this nice fairy and show gratitude for her kindness. According to the *Book of Post-Han Dynasty: Records of Prefectures and States*, "The woman Du Jiang can communicate with gods, the county thought her as a demon, she was confined in the prison, but she changed her shape and disappeared. An indictment was filed, people set up

每逢农历三月初三，江都古镇的人们蜂拥至庙场，大街小巷，人潮涌动，节日的欢乐气氛感染着每一位在场的老百姓。按照当地的传统，三月三是仙女庙的传统节日。江都的仙女庙在汉晋以前都被叫做"龙川"，据说从前在这条河里出过一条飞仙的小白龙，所以又叫做"白龙川"。据说这里有一位仙女曾经为战国时代的伍子胥指过路，功成名就的伍子胥为了感谢仙女的恩德，就在这里修建了一座庙宇供奉这位善良的仙女。《后汉书·郡国志》载："女子杜姜，左道通神，县以为妖，闭狱桎梏，卒变形，莫知所终，以状上，因以其地立庙，号曰东陵圣母"。

《酉阳杂俎》载："扬州东陵圣母，庙主女道士康紫霞侍奉圣母多年，一旦白日飞升，化为白龙而去"，所以实际上仙女庙是供奉女道士杜姜和她的徒弟康紫霞，称她们为"东陵圣母"。

a temple in her place, and called her Dongling Holy Mother." *Miscellaneous Morsels from Youyang* recorded that, "There was Dongling Holy Mother in Yangzhou, a female Taoist who was the temple chief served the Holy Mother for many years, she flew into the sky one day, and turned into a white dragon and flew away", so Fairy Temple was dedicated to Du Jiang and her disciple Kang Zixia, and people called them "Holy Mothers of Dongling".

The temple fair on March 3rd is related to the story of fairy salvation.

It was said that the country was in chaos because of the revolt of Wang Mang, Liu Xiu who was the ninth generation of the First Emperor of the Han Dynasty was chased by Wang Mang to the area of Fairy Temple (which was called Cai Village) on March 3rd, and was saved by a fisherman. Hereafter, the villagers built Golden Dragon Temple to show gratitude to the blessing of Liu Xiu (the villagers thought that the emperor was the embodiment of a golden dragon), and villagers from all directions came to burn incense and worship on March 3rd every year afterwards, and it was involved into temple fair.

All people get together in towns on March 3rd temple fair every year, and the scene is magnificent. Some people sell snacks, some people perform street monkeys, and some people strike gongs and drums, and various kinds of sounds make a fair symphony. In front of the Fairy Temple, pilgrimages come from all directions to burn incense and worship Dongling Holy Mothers, and pray for blessing of holy spirits. When temple fair begins, people shall offer incense at first.

When the offering of incense begins, the long line sets out. There are full of loud sounds of gongs, drums and firecrackers. "A horse" (a man acting as the divine horse) strips to his waist and wears red

三月三的庙会与仙女救恩的故事也有关系。

据说, 西汉末年, 王莽造反, 天下大乱, 三月初三, 汉高祖第九代孙刘秀被王莽追逃到仙女庙 (当时称蔡家庄) 一带, 为一渔夫所救。后来, 庄民感念刘秀的福泽, 特建一金龙王庙 (乡民以为皇帝是金龙化身), 以后每年三月三, 都有四乡八镇的村民前来烧香朝拜, 渐而演化成庙会。

每年的三月三庙会, 男女老少都赶到镇上, 场面相当壮观。有卖小吃的, 有耍猴的, 有敲锣打鼓的, 各种声音汇成一曲动听的交响乐。在仙女庙前, 香客们从四面八方来烧香祭拜东陵圣母, 祈求神灵保佑。庙会开始后, 要先行香。

行香开始, 浩浩荡荡的队伍起程了。只听锣鼓喧天, 鞭炮震响。"马匹" (充神马的人) 赤着上身, 穿红裤, 脸涂花纹，口中横衔一枝长铁签（代马嚼口），手执四五尺长的铁棍，在神前跪拜踊跃，挥舞开道。其后是香火队，信徒们背着香袋，手执香火，排成4行，徐徐而行。只见烟雾缭绕，缥缈弥漫，如入仙境一般。紧随香火队之后是鼓乐队，乐师身穿青衫，腰束黄带，手执鼓、拔、笙、箫、弦子、二胡等乐器，演奏乐曲。接下来，是人数最多的化妆的歌舞队，各种歌舞争奇斗胜，美不胜收。

要木头戏的人则靠一根扁担，扛着一个小台子，周围有布挡，上面挂有一排排尺把长的小木偶，台前挂有一个小布帘，艺人在布挡下面一手牵引线，一手敲大锣，嘴里唱着台词，台上的小木偶就绘声绘色地表演起来，什么《猪八戒招亲》、《孙悟空三打白骨精》……集生、旦、净、末、丑和文场、武场于一身，其景令人陶醉。

trousers, his face is painted with patterns, his mouth holds a long iron stick (symbolizing a harness), his hand holds an iron stick as long as four or five *chi*, and he is active in kneeling and worshiping in front of gods and waves the stick to open up the road. He is followed by the incense team, the disciples carry perfume satchels on their backs, hold incense in their hands, and walk slowly in four lines. The air is loaded with smoke, which is like a fairy land. The incense team is followed by the drum band, the musicians wear black clothes with yellow strips on their waists, they hold the musical instruments such as drums, cymbals, *sheng*, *xiao*, *xuanzi* and *erhu* etc. and perform music. Next, the make-up dance team has the largest quantity, and various kinds of songs and dances are charming and beautiful.

The performer who plays puppets carries a small platform, which is surrounded by a cloth shed, the lines of the puppets are hung in the front, and there is a small curtain in the front of the platform, the performer drags the lines under the cloth shed with one hand, and strikes a gong with another hand, he sings dialogs, and the puppets on the platform perform the plays vividly, such as *Pigsy's Marriage* and *Monkey King Conquers the White Boned Demon*, which integrate the male lead, the female lead, the painted face, the old man and the clown, the literal scene and the martial scene, which are attractive.

People who escape from disasters walk at the end of the team offering incense, who wear red prison garments, mumble, and kneel in evrey three steps, bow in every five steps, show gratitude to divine favors, and pray for blessing and peace. The team offering incense beats drums and blows trumpet, the atmosphere is lively, people stop after walking for a while and walk again after stopping for a while, walk around the town slowly and then go back to Dragon King Temple, and it's sunset now...

走在行香队伍最后的，是那些逢大难不死的劫后余生者，他们身穿大红囚衣，口里喃喃念语，三步一跪，五步一叩，感谢神明恩宠，祈祷保佑平安。行香队伍吹吹打打，热热闹闹，行一程停一阵，停一阵行一程，缓缓地绕镇一周后再折回龙王庙，这时已是红日偏西……

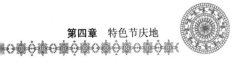

对于普通老百姓来说，三月三也是赶集的好时间。各地商贾都在这里云集，各种货品、农产品、土特产等都在市场上广受欢迎，应有尽有。夜晚的江都镇，灯火辉煌，人们在热闹的茶座和剧场里欣赏各类表演，不知不觉中爱上了这个充满灵气的小镇！庙会过后，陌生人成为了朋友；朋友之间感情更加深厚，江都也成为一个让人流连忘返的古镇！

As for common people, March 3rd is the good time for going to the market. Businessmen coming from all places get together here, various kinds of goods, agricultural articles and special products etc. are popular in the market, and all things are provided. Lights in Jiangdu Town are brilliant at night, people appreciate all kinds of performances in lively teahouses and theaters, and they fall in love in this ethereal town unconsciously! After the temple fair, strangers become friends; feeling between friends becomes deeper, and Jiangdu has become a fascinating ancient town!

2 黎族非物质文化遗产：三月三
Li People's Intangible Culture Heritage: March 3rd

Li people in Hainan Island always hold activities to commemorate their brave ancestors, and pursue beautiful love and happiness on March 3rd. Therefore, March 3rd is also called Love Festival or Love Day. The historical literature of the Song Dynasty recorded the celebration activity of March 3rd, and Fan Chengda's *Well-Balanced Records of Guihai* in the Song Dynasty wrote that, "There is Swing Fair in spring, men and women in neighboring areas dress up and go outing, they sing songs in antiphonal style hand in hand and shoulder to shoulder, which is called making play".

海南岛的黎族同胞在三月三的时候会举行活动纪念勇敢的祖先，追求美好的爱情和幸福。因此，三月三又被称为爱情节、谈爱日。早在宋代的史籍中就记录了三月三的庆祝活动，宋范成大《桂海虞衡志》云："春则秋千会，邻峒男女装束来游，携手并肩，互歌互答，名曰作剧。"

三月三节的来历还有一种说法。相传在很久以前，石洞有一只作恶多端的乌鸦精，使黎民百姓不得安居乐业。一天乌鸦精抓到了美丽的黎族少女俄娘，这年三月三，俄娘的心上人阿贵带尖刀弓箭上山救俄娘，被乌鸦精害死。俄娘闻讯悲痛万分，趁乌鸦精熟睡之机杀死了它，为阿贵报了仇，为黎族百姓除了大害。俄娘终生未嫁，每年农历三月三这一天她都会到俄贤洞唱她和阿贵恋爱时的情歌。后来，黎族人民为了纪念她，把这山洞取名为俄娘洞（昌江）。每年三月三这一天，附近的未婚黎族青年男女都会在俄贤岭集会，唱着情歌寻找自己的意中人。此项活动逐年扩大并传播至海南各个黎胞居住区，在海南黎胞中形成盛大的传统节日。

也有人说，三月三是为了纪念黎族的祖先"黎母"诞生、庆祝黎族人民幸福生活而举行的节日。每到这一天，黎族人

It was said that there was an evil crow spirit in a cave and made troubles for Li people long ago. One day, the crow spirit caught a beautiful Li maid whose name was E'niang, Agui who was the lover of E'niang brought a sharp knife, bows and arrows and came to the mountain to save her, but he was killed by the crow spirit. E'niang got the news, she was broken-hearted and killed it when it slept soundly, revenged for Agui, and got rid of the great disaster for Li people. She didn't marry in her life, and she came to E'xian Cave to sing the love songs which she sang with Agui when they fell in love on March 3rd every year. Afterwards, Li people called the cave E'niang Cave (Changjiang) in order to commemorate her. On March 3rd every year, nearby unmarried young men and women get together in E'xian Ridge and sing love songs to look for their favorite lovers. The activity has been enriched year by year, and has been spread to other areas which Li people inhabit, and has formed the grand traditional festival among Li people in Hainan.

Some people say that March 3rd is the festival for Li people to commemorate the birth of the ancestor "Li Mother" and celebrate their happy life. On this day, Li people dress up to take part in March 3rd song fair, bring Shanlan wine and bamboo tube rice and get together. In the evening, young men and girls burn bonfire to begin the celebration activities, play the national traditional dances such as bamboo dance and areca dance etc., and use songs and dances to express mutual feelings. If the feeling of two persons is harmonious, they exchange gifts with each other, young girls tie seven-colored girdles, which are made by themselves, on waists of young men, and young men tie love tokens made by themselves to young girls.

Various kinds of sports activities attract attention of many sports fans, tourists also take part in these activities such as wrestling, tug-of-war, shooting and swing, and people enjoy themselves happily and express their love to life with songs and dances and their pursuit to romance. Hainai, the areas in which Li people inhabit, holds grand celebration activities on March 3rd every year, which attract many tourists from afar to watch celebration programs.

民就穿上盛装参加三月三歌会，带着山兰酒和竹筒饭，聚集在一起。晚上，男女青年烧起熊熊篝火开始欢庆活动，跳起竹竿舞、槟榔舞等民族传统舞蹈，用歌声和舞姿来诉说对彼此的感情。如果双方感情融洽，还互赠礼物，姑娘们将自己亲手编织而成的七彩腰带系在小伙子腰间，小伙子也拿出自己给姑娘制作的定情信物。

除此之外，还有各种体育活动也吸引不少体育爱好者，像摔跤、拔河、射击、荡秋千这些活动都不断地有游人积极参与，人们尽情地欢庆着，用歌声和舞蹈表达对生活的热爱，对爱情的追求。现在每年的三月三，海南的黎族聚居区都要举办盛大的庆祝活动，吸引了不少远方的游客来观看庆祝节目。

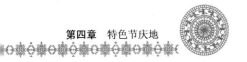

3 乌江镇的三月三

March 3rd of Wujiang Town

"生当做人杰，死亦为鬼雄。至今思项羽，不肯过江东。"西楚霸王的故事是人们耳熟能详的，但是三月三为什么又和楚霸王联系在一起呢？在安徽和县乌江镇，当地人代代相传着关于楚霸王的故事。据《和县志》记载，项羽自刎之后，当即被汉将瓜分遗体。当地百姓就地掩埋了残骸和血衣，是为"衣冠冢"。后人于此建亭祭祀，人称"项亭"。于唐代始建祠，上元三年，由唐代书法家李阳冰为祠书写了篆额："西楚霸王灵祠"。历代文人墨客路过此地都

"If a person has to die, he should die for his country and thus becomes a ghost hero. People still remember Xiang Yu since he refused to flee across Wujiang River." People are familiar with the story of the Conqueror of Western Chu. How is March 3rd related to the King of Chu? The story of the Conqueror of Chu has been spread among local people in Wujiang Town, Hexian County of Anhui for generations. According to *Hexian County Records*, Xiang Yu's body was divided by generals of the Han after he committed suicide. Local people buried his remains and bloody clothes immediately to make a cenotaph for him. The later generations built the pavilion for sacrifice, which is called "Xiang Pavilion". The temple was built in the Tang Dynasty, Li Yangbing who was the calligrapher of the Tang Dynasty wrote "Divine Temple of the Conqueror of Chu" on the forehead of the temple. The men of letters of later dynasties passed the place, and leant against the rail to commemorate this great hero. Dai Zhong in the Ming Dynasty described the Conqueror Temple, "He stayed in Sparrow Temple, and the lonely boat anchored beside Wujiang River, the diseased leaves fell in the wind, and the cold wave didn't leave in the night." The story of "Crying of the Conqueror" had been spread in Hexian County.

According to *Record of the Listener* of Hong Mai of the Song Dynasty, Du Mo who was born in Hezhou failed in examinations successively. He had the air of freedom, he was drunk in the Temple of the Conqueror Xiang beside Wujiang River, he burned incense and bowed in front of the Conqueror, then he walked to his seat, held his neck, touched his head, cried loudly, "You have a companion now. Heroes like you cannot conquer the world, the articles of Du Mo are excellent, but I cannot be an official." He cried after finishing his words, and his tears flowed like a spring. The temple attendant worried that he would be punished, forced him to withdraw from the hall, Du Mo still sighed and couldn't release his feeling. When the attendant held the candle to inspect the divine statue, it also shed the tears.

Du Mo, whose name was Du Shixiong, was the "song sage" of the Song Dynasty, and won his reputation with "the Ci(lyric poetry) sage" Ouyang Xiu and the "poem sage" Shi Manqin. He failed successively in examinations, and he felt frustrated.

要凭栏吊唁这位伟大的英雄。明代诗人戴重在诗中描写霸王祠："夕阳留雀庙，孤艇系乌江，病叶相风残，寒潮夜不降。"在和县当地，流传着"哭霸王"的故事。

据宋代洪迈《夷坚志》载：和州人杜默，累举不成名。性英俍不羁，因为乌江谒项王庙，被酒沾醉，方柱香拜讫，径升偶座，据神颈，拊其首而恸，大声语曰：大王有相亏者，英雄如大王而不得天下，文章如杜默而进取不得官。语毕又大恸，泪如迸泉。庙祝虑其获罪，强扶以下，掖之而出，犹回首嗟叹不能自释。祝秉烛检视，神像亦垂泪未已。

杜默，名杜师雄，是宋代的一代"歌豪"，与"词豪"欧阳修、"诗豪"石曼卿齐名。然而早年屡中不第，苦恼万分。因此回到故乡，来到霸王祠前就触动心事，抱着霸王塑像的头大哭了一场。神奇的是，霸王塑像也默默地流泪了。这真是古今同悲的一哭。如今，我们看到，在项羽塑像的立柱上，还有一则楹联写道："司马迁乃汉臣，本纪一篇不信史官无曲笔；杜师雄真豪士，灵祠大哭至今墓木有余悲。"

杜师雄就是和县人，晚年辞官回到故里，隐居于和县西南约20公里处的丰山杜村。他曾在屋前手植六株梅花，现存一株，稀奇的是，这株老梅，每年春天只开半边花，还有半边到下一年才开，轮番开放。被当地人称为"宋时梅"，又叫"半枝梅"。

每年三月三，按照当地的习俗，人们在霸王祠前举办庙会，届时除了传统的赶集之外，还有各种文化活动，例如龙灯队、高跷队及庐剧表演，还

Therefore, he returned to his hometown.He was touched when coming to the Conqueror Temple, and cried on the shoulder of the statue of the Conqueror. The statue of the Conqueror cried magically. This was the sad symphony of the old and the new. At present, we can see the couplet on the pillars of the statue of Xiang Yu, "Sima Qian was the courtier of the Han, the record of the historian didn't distort the facts; Du Shixiong was heroic, his cry in the temple had made the tomb wood sad till now."

Du Shixiong was born in Hexian County, he returned to his hometown after the resignation in his old age, and lived in seclusion in Fengshandu Village which was about 20 kilometers in southwest of Hexian County. He planted six plum trees in front of his house, and there exist only an old one today, it blooms in a semi-circle, another semi-circle will bloom in the next year, and the two circles bloom in turn. The local people calle it "Song Plum" as well as "Semi-circle Plum".

According to the local convention on March 3rd every year, people hold the temple fair in front of the Conqueror Temple. Besides traditional custom of going to market, there are many cultural activities such as dragon lantern team, stilts team and Luzhou opera performance, programs including patrol of the

Conqueror etc. Nearby township common people come to burn incense and commemorate this hero. "March 3rd Temple Fair of the King Temple" has been listed as a Intengible culture heritage in the first nominees by Jiangsu Provincial Government today.

有霸王出巡等节目。附近乡镇的老百姓也都纷纷赶来烧香祭奠这位英雄。现"霸王祠三月三庙会"已被江苏省政府列为首批非物质文化遗产。

4 侗家的"播种节"

Dong People's Seed Sowing Festival

在贵州黔东南自治州镇远县报京乡，当地侗族同胞有自己独特的庆祝三月三的方式。三月三在当地又被称之为"播种节"。一种说法是因为农历的三月本来就是农忙播种的季节，为了秋季能有好收成，村民们在这个时候祭祀祖先和各路神灵，希望他们能够保佑庄稼顺利成熟。春暖花开的时候，也是男女青年播种爱情的时候，他们借此机会互相认识、了解，在歌声和舞蹈中了解彼此，增进感情。

In Baojing Village, Zhenyuan Town, Autonomous Prefecture of southeastern Guizhou, local Dong people celebrate March 3rd in a unique way. March 3rd is called "Sowing Festival" locally. There is a saying that lunar March is the busy season of sowing, and villagers sacrifice to ancestors and gods in order to get good harvest at this time of the year, and hope that they can bless the ripening of crops. Young men and women sow love in spring, they take the chance to know each other, acquaint each other in the ways of songs and dances, and express their feelings.

March 3rd is also a memorial date of love tragedy in the local legend.

Long long ago, the household of Zhou Laoshun who was a Dong peasant lived in Baojing Village, Zhenyuan County, Guizhou Province. The couple had a daughter in their forties, whose name was Liangying. The girl learnt to weave and embroider from her mother. Dong cloth with pepper and flowers woven by her, and the five-colored Dong brocade embroidered by her were paid as tributes of Dong Village to the capital. Liangying had been a famous ingenious girl in Baojing Village.

A young man named Liu Qiaosheng whose parents died when he was a child lived end beside the village's pool. He earned his living by doing farm works, cutting woods and capturing sparrows. Kind Mother Zhou took care of Qiaosheng and often sent something to this poor boy to eat and wear. Qiaosheng often came to Zhou's family to cut wood, plough fields, thrash and carry grains. As time flew, Qiaosheng called Mother Zhou and Father Zhou as adoptive parents and became the good and inseparable friend of Liangying. When they were seven or eight years old, they fell in love secretly.

在当地的传说中，三月三也还是一个爱情悲剧的纪念日呢。

很久很久以前，贵州省镇远县报京寨上住着侗族农户周老顺一家。夫妻俩四十开外时，喜得独女，名良英。良英姑娘自幼跟妈妈学会了纺织刺绣。她织的胡椒眼提花侗布，绣的五彩侗锦，总被选作侗乡贡品，进贡京城。良英成了报京寨里鼎鼎有名的巧姑娘。

寨脚大塘边住着一个从小就没了爹娘的孤儿，名叫刘桥生。这后生靠自己种地、砍柴、捕雀过日子。善良的周大妈见到桥生总是问寨问暖的，逢年过节，还常常匀点吃的、穿的接济这个穷孩子。桥生也常来周家帮着砍柴、犁田、打谷、挑粮。日子长了，桥生便认周大妈为干妈，叫周老顺干爹，和良英也成了形影不离的好朋友。长到七、八岁的时候，他和良英悄悄爱慕上了。

桥生和良英的心事哪能瞒得过周大妈?老两口真是又高兴又发愁。对桥生这个干儿子，他们打心眼里喜欢，可寨子里有"还娘头"的族规：姑妈的长女必须嫁给舅爹的儿子。良英舅爹的儿子二十出头了，正等着接亲了。再说，良英的舅爹又是报京一带九个侗寨的寨头，这族规岂是随便改得了的?想到这一层，老两口饭不香，觉不甜，只怕是眼前这对鸳鸯要散啊。

翻过年进了正月，冰冻山野，寒风刺骨，舅爹派媒婆带了聘礼上周家给良英提亲来了。周老顺推说良英不在家。媒婆叫嚷说："聘礼已下，你少啰嗦。三月三接亲，一言为定。"说罢，转身走出门。

当晚，周大妈和良英归来，见到那聘礼，良英哭着直喊："我不去，我不去!"望着女儿，除了流泪，实在想不出一点办法。母女俩抱头痛哭。

Qiaosheng and Liangying cannot hide their worries from Mother Zhou! The old couple were pleased and worried. They genuinely liked Qiaosheng, the adoptive son, but the village had the convention of "Returning to Maternal Family", i.e. the first daughter of aunt will marry the son of the maternal uncle. The son of the uncle of Liangying ,who was in his twenties, was waiting for the marriage. The uncle of Liangying was the chief of nine villages in Baojing, and it was uneasy to change the clan rule. Thinking about it, the old couple couldn't eat well, and feared that the lovers wouldl be separated.

In January of that year, the mountain fields were frozen, the cold wind penetrated one's bones, and the uncle assigned a woman matchmaker to go to Zhou's family to propose a marriage with betrothal presents. Zhou Laoshun explained that Liangying wasn't at home. The matchmaker said loudly, "We have sent the betrothal gifts. Don't chatter on and on. We will fetch the bride on March 3rd." After saying the words, she turned away.

When Mother Zhou and Liangying returned home, they saw the betrothal gifts. Liangying cried, "I don't want to marry! I don't want to marry!" Seeing the daughter, the mother couldn't find a solution except crying. The mother and the daughter cried together.

It was at dusk of March 2nd the matchmaker led six young men who carried wine, meat and glutinous rice to present gifts to Zhou's family. Zhou Laoshun and his wife were forced to smile and received them. Liangying was in the house and said the words, "I don't want to marry to the family of the uncle." Mother Zhou knew the feeling of her daughter, and said to Liangying, "You can ask Qiaosheng to come to our house and reunite with him for the last night." Liangying nodded. Qiaosheng came after a while. Liangying came out to see him and her feeling was mixed with joys and sorrows. Thinking that Liangying will be forced to the family of her uncle in the next morning, Qiaosheng bore his sadness and pain, he sang farewell songs to depart from Liangying in antiphonal style. The bride had to dress up just before dawn, so Qiaosheng left at midnight. On the way home, he came to the old Moga tree beside Jintang Cave. When he and Liangying fell in love, they often met with each other under this big tree. Qiaosheng couldn't help sighing deeply when he saw the evergreen ancient tree and thought that he would depart from Liangying forever. Suddenly, Qiaosheng heard the sound of steps, he turned back and saw Liangying carrying a basket on her back, holding a bamboo basket in her hand and walking towards him in a hurry. "Adoptive brother!" "Liangying, you…" Qiaosheng was surprised and pleased. Liangying held Qaiosheng, "I would rather die than marry the family of my uncle, we shall be

转眼就到了三月初二。黄昏时分，媒婆领着六名挑酒、挑肉、挑糯米饭的后生，到周家过礼来了。周老顺夫妇强装笑脸，出面应酬。良英在房里，还是那句老话："舅爹家，我不去，我不去，我不去！"周大妈懂得女儿的心意，对良英说："去接桥生来团聚最后一晚吧！"良英点了点头。不一会，桥生来了。良英出房相陪，心里却像打翻了的五味瓶，辨不清酸甜苦辣。桥生想到良英明天一早就要被迫嫁到舅爹家去，便忍着悲痛，和良英对歌告别。五更天新嫁娘要梳妆出嫁，桥生三更时分就告别离开了。回家路上，他不由自主地来到了金塘洞边那棵年高寿长的莫嘎树下。当初，他和良英相好时，常在这棵大树下相会。眼看古树常绿，良英却要永远分离，桥生不禁深深地叹了口气。突然间，桥生听见脚步响，回头一看，只见良英身背一个笆篓，手提一只竹篮，急匆匆地走了过来。

"干哥。""良英，你……"桥生又惊又喜。良英拉着桥生说："舅爹家我死也不去，干哥，我俩永远在一起。我们趁早离开这里，苗岭这么宽，总有我俩的栖身处，侗家这么多，总有人欢迎我们。"

桥生见良英对自己这么忠贞，感动得不知说什么才好。良英又说："干哥，你把左脚鞋脱下，我把右脚鞋脱下，在莫嘎树上印下我俩的一对脚印，请年高寿长的莫嘎树给我们作媒证婚。"桥生点点头。于是，两人各脱下一只鞋，在莫嘎树上印下了一对并排的脚印。良英取下笆篓给桥生，说："笆篓里装的是我早晨捞的鲜鲤鱼，我们带着它，愿一路上百事如意，年年有余。"桥生接过笆篓拷在腰间，伸手向良英要竹篮，说："良英，那篮葱蒜让我提。愿我们到了远方福地，我的秧苗像葱一样肯发篼，长的稻杆像蒜苗那样粗壮，岁岁丰收，

together forever. Miao Ridge is so wide that we can find a place to live. There are so many Dong people, some of whom will welcome us."

Qiaosheng saw the loyalty of Liangying, he was touched greatly. Liangying said, "Adoptive brother. You take off your left shoe, I take off my right shoe, and we leave a pair of footprints on the Moga tree and ask the old Moga tree to be our matchmaker and marriage witness." Qiaosheng nodded. Therefore, they took off one of their shoes, and left a pair of parallel footprints on the Moga tree. Liangying took down the basket, gave it to Qiaosheng and said, "This is the fresh carp I caught in the morning, we bring it and hope that everything is OK on our way, and we have surplus year after year." Qiaosheng received the basket and hung it on his waist, stretched out his hand to Liangying for the bamboo basket.He said, "Liangying! Let me carry the onion and garlic basket. I hope that seedlings planted by us will grow as prosperous as onion, and stalks will grow as strong as garlic, we will have a bumper harvest every year, and our life will be beautiful in the blessed land afar." Saying the words, Qiaosheng took the bamboo basket, and ran out of the village with Liangying and disappeared in the distance.

When the cock crowed for the third time in the village, it was just before dawn. The matchmaker hastened the bride to dress up for the marriage, but she didn't see Liangying and asked people to look for her everywhere in the village, but they couldn't find her. After the dawn, all people of Baojing Village crowded to Jintang Cave, and came to the Moga tree under which Qiaosheng and Liangying met with each other, only saw a pair of footprints left by them…They fled to a faraway place. The courage with which they resisted against feudalism had impression on young Baojing Dong men and women deeply like the pair of footprints on the Moga tree.

Hereafter, young men and girls who play Lusheng dance come to the Moga tree, look at the footprints left by Qiaosheng and Liangying, young Dong men come to Jintang Cave, ask baskets with onion and garlic from their sweet lovers, engage affections mutually, and express their feelings with each other. This is the origin of "March 3rd" of Dong people[1].

①Collection of Chinese Folk Customs and Sources (Volume of Holidays and Seasons), pp154-156.

化活美好。"说着，桥生接过竹篮，和良英双双奔出寨外，直向远方。

再说寨里，鸡叫三遍，已到五更。媒婆催促新娘梳妆出嫁，进绣房张望，没见良英，喊人到寨上四处找寻，也没见新娘的身影。天明以后，报京寨男女老少拥到金塘洞边——桥生、良英常约会的莫嘎树下，只见树干上留着他俩的一对脚印……桥生和良英远走高飞了。他俩那种反对封建族规的勇气，就像莫嘎树上那对脚印一样，深深地印在报京侗家后生和姑娘们的心坎上。

以后，每到三月三这天，男女青年都要跳着芦笙舞来到莫嘎树下，瞻仰桥生、良英留下的脚印，侗家后生都要到金塘洞边，向自己心爱的情妹讨芭篓，讨葱篮，互相定情，共表衷心。这就是侗族"三月三"的来历①。

①雪犁等主编，《中华民俗源流集成（节日岁时卷）》，甘肃人民出版社，1994年，第154-156页

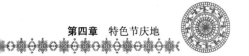

如今的"三月三"节是全寨人请客会友的节日，按照报京的习俗，只有"三月三"的三天，青年男女才能在屋里唱情歌，其他的日子只能在山坡上唱。过了三月三，寨上的芦笙都要封存起来，直到谷子全部进仓以后，芦笙才能开封。

March 3rd is the festival for all villagers to entertain guests and meet friends. According to the convention of Baojing, young men and girls can only sing love songs in houses during the three days of "March 3rd", and they can sing songs on slopes on other dates. After March 3rd, all *lusheng* of the villages shall be kept and they can be opened only if all millets are put into barns.

5 荔枝湾，三月三
March 3rd of Lizhiwan

There is a district named Liwan which has very profound culture in Guangzhou,and it can be traced back to the Western Han Dynasty with the history of over two thousand years. Liwan has been a good leisure place for local people for a long time, imperial families and celebrities built gardens here and men of letters often visited here historically. There was an old saying, "March 3rd of Lizhiwan", and people go to visit Liwan on March 3rd. Liwan District began to hold Renwei Temple Fair of Pantang since 2005.

Renwei Temple in Pantang of Liwan District is the Taoist temple to worship the Northern Emperor,villagers hold activities such as temple fair,moving god, playing operas etc.on lunar March 3rd to celebrate the birthday of the Northern Emperor and pray for good harvest. The Northern Emperor,

广州有一个文化底蕴非常深厚的荔湾城区，其历史可以追溯到西汉时期，至今已有两千多年的历史了。长期以来，荔湾都是当地人民休闲的好去处，历史上历代皇家名流都在这里修建花园，文人墨客也经常在这里流连。旧时也有俗语说"三月三，荔枝湾"，人们在三月三的时候到荔湾来游玩。荔湾区在2005年开始举办"三月三泮塘仁威庙会"。

荔湾区泮塘的仁威庙是供奉北帝的道教庙宇，每逢农历三月初三北帝诞时，村民举办庙会、游神、唱戏等庆祝活动，祈求一年风调雨顺。北帝，全称北方真武玄天上帝，其又有玄天、玄天上帝、武大帝、真武大帝、北极大帝、北极佑圣真君、开天大帝、元武神等称号，是道教供奉的神。

相传，北帝原本是古净乐国王的太子，生而神猛，越东海来游，遇天神授以宝剑，入湖北武当山修炼，经四十二年而功成，白日飞升，威镇北方，号玄武君。宋讳玄字，因称真武。宋赵彦卫《云麓漫钞》卷九："朱雀、玄武、青龙、白虎，为四方之神。祥符间避圣祖讳，始改玄武。后兴醴泉观，得龟蛇。"道士以为真武观，绘其像为北方之神。其为统理北方、统领所有水族(故兼水神)之道教民间神祇，又称黑帝。据说拥有消灾解困，治水御火及延年益寿的神力，故颇受拥戴。据《太上说玄天大圣真武本传神咒妙经》，北帝是太上老君第八十二次变化之身，托生于大罗境上无欲天宫，为净乐国王及善胜皇后之子。皇后梦而吞日，

whose full name is the Northern Zhenwu Heavenly Superior Emperor, is also titled as the Heavenly, Heavenly Superior Emperor, Wu Emperor, Zhenwu Emperor, North-pole Emperor, North-pole Holy Emperor, Heaven Creating Emperor, and Yuanwu God etc.,and is the Taoist god.

As the story goes, the Northern Emperor was the prince of ancient King Jingle ,and he was so brave and furious,crossed East Sea,met a god who gave a treasured sword to him, came to Wudang Mountain in Hubei Province to cultivate vital energy. He became an immortal forty-two years later, flew into sky in the daytime,was famous in the north,and was titled as Lord Xuanwu. Xuan of Xuanwu a was forbidden word in the Song Dynasty, so he was renamed Zhenwu. According to Volume 9 of *Yunlu Manchao* written by Zhao Yanwei in the Song Dynasty, "Zhuque,Xuanwu,Qinglong and Baihu were four gods in four directions. In order to avoid the taboo of the holy ancestor in the years of Xiangfu, Xuanwu was changed initially. When Sweet Spring Temple was built afterwards, snakes and turtles were obtained." Taoists thought that temple was dedicated to Zhenwu, so painted his image as the Northern God. He was the folk Taoist god governing all water tribes in the noth(was the Water God), and was also called the Black Emperor. It was said that he had the divine power to get rid of misfortune and difficulty, prevent flood and fire, and prolong life, so he was supported greatly.According to *Superior Mantra and Sutra on the Heavenly and*

Holy Zhenwu, the Northern Emperor was the 82nd transformation of the Superior Lord, was born in Desireless Palace of All-Embracing Realm, and was the son of King Jingle and Queen Shansheng. The queen swallowed the sun in her dream, then was pregnant, delivered him in the palace after over fifteen months. After he grew up, he left his parents,came to Wudang Mountain to cultivate himself, and became an immortal forty-two years later and flew into the sky in the daytime. The Jade Emperor gave the imperial edict to entitle him as Taixuan and let him govern the north.

Cantonese live by sea and live on sea fishing, people worship the Northern Emperor who was the Water God, and ask him for harvest of local agriculture and fishery. The birthday celebration in Pantang Village is also called "Zhenwu Fair",the grand patrol of the Northern Emperor is held during the period, which is also called God Patrol. When the Northern Emperor patrols, two gong players open a way, the god is carried by people, he patrols in streets and lanes, people beat drums and clang

觉而怀孕，经一十四月及四百余辰，降诞于王宫。后既长成，遂舍家辞父母，入武当山修道，历42年功成果满，白日升天。玉皇大帝有诏，封为太玄，镇于北方。

广东人依海生存，出海捕鱼谋生，而北帝又是水神，人们崇敬北帝，祈求北帝能给当地农业和渔业带来丰收。泮塘村的北帝诞又叫做"真武会"，其间还有盛大的北帝巡游，又叫"神斗巡游"。神斗是一个宫殿，里面安放着刻有"北方真武玄天上帝"字样的神主牌匾。北帝出巡的时候，由两个铜锣手开路，然后由人把神斗抬出来，巡游至大街小巷，一边敲锣打鼓表示吉祥喜庆，人们在自己家门口烧

香磕头。巡游结束之后，还有神功戏歌颂北帝的功德，非常热闹，气氛也相当热烈。

"三月三，荔枝湾"的内容相当丰富，有转文塔、逛庙会、会男女、游船河、乐童玩、睇大戏、对诗画、叹美食、拎手信、派福米等各个项目，除此之外，还有老广州生活百态展示、木偶戏等吸引游客眼球的活动。

1、转文塔

这也是三月三的一个重头戏，荔枝湾的文塔是广州市区内唯一的功名塔，有四百多年历史，据传广东清代三个状元都曾到此拜祭过后上京赶考科举中魁的，其中的梁耀枢还住在不远处，即西关的陶陶居附近，还有清代的探花李文田也住过附近的恩宁路，现仍有其故居泰华楼，可见西关荔枝湾一带的文运的兴盛。由于新中国成立前文塔就荒废已久，有关的记载和记忆都甚少，故根据各地文塔和泮塘乡民拜文昌的习俗，重点恢复了转文塔祈愿的民

gongs to show auspiciousness and happiness. After the completion of the patrol, lively divine operas praise the virtues of the Northern Emperor, and the atmosphere is fervent.

"March 3rd of Lizhiwan" has rich contents, including going to Literary Tower, holding temple fairs, dating lovers, boating, children's playing games, watching opera, poems and paintings, delicious foods, bringing presents and sending gifts etc., and many splendid activitives such as displaying life of old Guangzhou and puppet show etc. can attract tourists.

1. Going to Literary Tower

This is one of the important programs on March 3rd. Literary Tower of Lizhiwan is the unique tower of honor and power and has a history of over four hundred years. It was said that three scholars in the Qing Dynasty came to the capital to participate in imperial examinations and became Number One Scholars after sacrificing and worshipping. Liang Yaoshu of the three scholars lived near Xiguan's Taotao Residence, and Li Wentian, Number Two Scholar in the Qing Dynasty, lived near Enning Road, and his former home Taihua Building has been kept till now, which shows flourishing literature in the area of Lizhiwan of Xiguan. Because Literary Tower had been ruined for a long time, there were few relevant records and memories, so the activity orients at restoring common people who go to Literary Tower to make wishes according to the conventions of other literary towers and Pantang villagers worshiping Wenchang. This is the first formal re-initiation of the gate of Literary Tower for many years, so there is a special opening ceremony. Residents of the city and tourists can go to Literary Tower to make wishes, they can visit the tower, get local presents with special significance, and once it opens up, residents of the city and tourists can apply for participation in visiting Literary Tower and being given presents on the opening ceremony day. Prayers with "literary gifts",i.e.onion, celery and *zongzi* follow the Wisdom Star to go around Literary Tower. According to the traditional saying, "onion, celery and *zongzi*" symbolize "cleverness, diligence and success".

2. Strolling about Temple Fair

Renwei Temple Fair of Pantang is the core program on March 3rd, which has been reserved completely and extended its duration nowadays, the believers can come into the temple to worship the Northern Emperor and make wishes, and there are performances such as acrobatics, comic dialogue, conjuring, oral stunts, Cantonese opera, Cantonese songs, singing and dancing and folk music etc., and the most passionate and splendid programs are the lion teams' meeting of Xijiao Village and its neighbouring three villages, waking lion patrol, authentic martial arts and dancing dragon

众，这也是文塔大门许多年来的首次正式重启，开幕式上有一个很特别的文塔开启仪式，此后每天市民游客都可来转文塔祈愿，并可进塔内参观许愿，同时还可拿到具有特别意义的地道民俗的手信，开幕式当天还将开放部分名额让市民游客报名参加文塔观礼、拎手信。参与祈福的人们手拿着一份"文礼"——"葱、芹菜、粽子"，跟着"文曲星"开始转文塔。按照传统习俗的说法，"葱、芹菜、粽子"分别寓意着"聪明、勤奋、高中"。

2、逛庙会

泮塘仁威庙会是三月三的核心项目，被完全保留并延长了时间，期间信众可进庙拜北帝祈福许愿，庙外广场还有杂技、相声、魔术、口技、粤剧、粤曲、歌舞、民乐等演出，最激情壮观的是当天西郊乡及上下三村各友乡狮队的到访会狮和醒狮巡游，还有质朴的泮塘村民武术、舞龙表演，以及

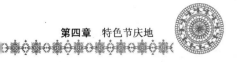

当天下午艺高人胆大的狮艺表演等。

3、会男女

古时三月三可以说是最早法定的情人节了，《周礼·地官·媒氏》中说："仲春之月，令会男女，于是时也，奔者不禁。"时至近代，三月三青年男女结伴踏青游春依然盛行。

4、游船河

游船河是荔枝湾传统的游玩消闲项目，荔枝湾涌的治理恢复也让这一历史经典得以恢复，三月三期间，荔枝湾游船时间从早上9：30一直到晚上的9：30，市民游客还可能会得到特别优惠或礼物。

5、乐童玩

部分岭南地区的童玩项目也恢复了，包括陀螺、滚铁圈、跳橡筋、跳格、弹波子、挑绳等十多种童玩游戏。

performance of Pantang villagers, and exquisite and bold lion art performance in the afternoon.

3. Dating

March 3rd in ancient times is the earliest legal Lover's day for dating. *The Rites of Zhou: Local Official: Matchmaker* wrote, "Men and women make dates in the middle of spring, and adultery isn't forbidden in the season." It's popular for young men and women to go outings together in spring on March 3rd in modern times.

4. Boating

Boating is the traditional recreation and leisure program of Lizhiwan, the treatment and restoration of Lizhiwan Brook restores the historical classic, boating time begins at 9:30 in the morning and ends at 9:30 in the evening during the period of March 3rd, residents of the city and tourists can get special discounts or presents.

5. Children's Playing Games

Over ten children's playing games in some Lingnan areas have been restored, including whipping top, rolling iron circle, jumping rubber string, jumping grids, playing balls, jumping rope and so on.

6. Watching Opera

Liwan is the hometown of Chinese operas, it has profound tradition of Cantonese operas and songs. Cantonese opera is performed nearly everyday during the period of March 3rd, Grand Pearl River Delta Cantonese Arts Performance is held on the square of Renwei Temple and the southern gate of Lizhiwan Park on the last day (April 6th), performance groups from various places compete for skills in turn, and fans of Cantonese operas and songs shall not miss them.

7. Poems and Paintings

Many calligraphers and painters will perform in front of audience in this time, and there are many puzzles with rewards.

8. Delicious Foods

There is no spring outing without foods on March 3rd, there are delicious foods in Guangzhou and delicious tastes in Xiguan, which was one of the reasons for people to go spring outing in Liwan. The famous Cantonese Gastronomist Garden is located beside Renwei Temple of Lizhiwan, which has the old and famous shops including Panxi Wineshop. During the period of March 3rd, famous gastronomists with their teams are invited to praise Xiguan gastronomy.

6、睇大戏

荔湾是中国戏曲之乡，粤剧粤曲民间基础深厚，三月三期间几乎每天都有粤剧表演，而最后一天（4月6日）更是全天在仁威庙广场和荔湾湖公园南门进行珠三角粤艺大汇演，各地表演队伍将轮番竞技，粤剧粤曲爱好者都很喜欢。

7、对诗画

这次也专门邀请多位书画家应众挥毫，现场还有灯谜、楹联等有奖竞猜。

8、叹美食

三月三游春少不了吃，食在广州，味在西关，这也是以前人们喜欢来荔湾游春的原因之一，荔枝湾仁威庙旁正是著名的广州美食园，有泮溪酒家等名老字号。三月三期间，请知名美食家带队细叹西关美食。

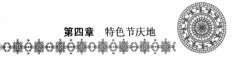

9、拎手信

广州话有说"吃夹拎"，游玩之余必带手信。三月三转文塔等民俗与手信结合的应节手信，让游人爱不释手。

10、派福米

这也是仁威庙会的必备项目，向区内特困群体派发生活物品，以彰显慈善公益事业。

"三月三，荔枝湾"是广州规模盛大的三月三民间活动了，让游客近距离感受岭南文化的魅力，也尽量让群众参与其中，展示出社会的和谐与欢乐。而且有一些内容是三月三活动特别的，例如转文塔仪式，以后看到拿笔和葱、芹菜等的就知道一定是去荔枝湾转文塔祈愿的了。

9. Bringing Presents

There is a Cantonese saying that "eating soup", and presents shall be brought when people travel and play. Seasonal presents integrate going to Literary Tower on March 3rd with presents, which make tourists be fond of them.

10. Sending Gifts

This is the necessary program of Renwei Temple Fair, and it distributes life necessities to the poor in the area in order to display charity and public welfare undertakings.

Generally speaking, they are March folk cultural activities at the largest scale today in Guangzhou, it is the first time to restore and display the traditional Lingnan spring outing and highlight local cultural characteristics. These activities make common people participate in them, pursue good wishes and feel happiness of social harmony. March 3rd is the unique activity in Guangzhou area, and there is a special ceremony for going to Literary Tower on the first day. Going to Literary Tower will be the important symbol of the beginning of March 3rd folk programs, and it will be known that people go to Lizhiwan's Literary Tower to make wishes from pens, onion and celery brought by them in the future.

"Color" ("Se") is a kind of typical folk art of Lingnan, including ethereal color, autumn color, water color, spring color and horse color etc., and the admirable folk arts such as ethereal color and water color etc. can be seen on the second day of Lizhiwan activities. March 3rd celebration activities promote local historical culture, and make tourists truly feel pure folk culture of Xiguan in Guangzhou.

"色"是岭南很典型的一种民间艺术，有飘色、秋色、水色、春色、马色等，荔枝湾三月三活动也有飘色、水色等举世无双的民间艺术，三月三的庆祝活动发掘了地方历史文化，让游客真正感受广州西关纯粹的民俗文化。

177

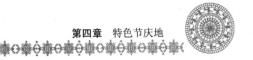

6 曲江上巳节
Winding River Shangsi Festival

2012年3月24日上午，西安大唐芙蓉园"上巳节"申报国家非物质文化遗产启动仪式在紫云楼举行。当天，大唐芙蓉园围绕上巳节申遗大会、全球女子成人礼及曲江流饮等活动的开展，让广大游客充分了解上巳节传统文化，共同为上巳节申请世界非物质文化遗产而努力。

曲江流饮作为上巳节千年传承的风俗，在大唐芙蓉园得到了较好的保护和传承。群贤毕至、曲江流饮已经成为上巳节文人雅士不可或缺的娱乐活动。大唐芙蓉园还邀请

The initiation ceremony of "Shangsi Festival" of Datang Hibiscus Garden of Xi'an which applied for national intangible cultural heritage was held in Ziyun Building on the morning of March 24th, 2012. Datang Hibiscus Garden developed the activities which oriented at Heritage Application of Shangsi Festival Conference, Global Women Coming-of-Age Ceremony, Winding Water and Floating Drinks, massive tourists fully knew about the traditional culture of Shangsi Festival and made common efforts to Shangsi Festival's application for World intangible Cultural Heritage.

The activity of winding water and floating drinks has become the convention of Shangsi Festival which has been passed down for one thousand years, and has been protected and inherited by Datang Hibiscus Garden. Assembling talented people, winding water and floating drinks have become necessary recreational activities of men

of letters and scholars in Shangsi Festival. Datang
Hibiscus Garden also invites many famous cultural
experts and scholars, who wear ancient clothes,
are seated on the ground, and compose poems with
graceful ancient Chinese zither performance, and the
splendid scene of winding water and floating goblets
reappears.

了众多知名文化专家、学
者，大家身着古装、席地
而坐，伴随着优雅的古琴
演奏吟诗作赋，再现曲水
流觞胜景。

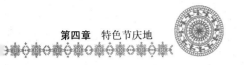

7 朝拜
Pilgrimage

十五和八月十五, 老百姓就带上粑粑、炒豆、香蜡纸烛去朝石宝山。这个朝拜仪式和鹤庆的来历有关。

相传, 很古的时候, 西藏王的大总管年尼有个儿子年伽陀, 是佛祖下凡, 从小精通佛经, 深得西藏王的宠爱。当时, 西藏王为了与白王结盟, 派年伽陀为使臣。年伽陀向班禅要了一串舍利子和年尼珠, 带起天生酒、藏葡萄、鳌犬、藏马、珍珠等礼品, 向大理出发了。

路过剑川东山、鹤庆西山的时候, 年伽陀见海子白茫茫一片, 就表示

Common people bring buns, fried beans, incenses, papers and candles to pilgrim to Shibao Mountain on March 15th and August 15th of the lunan calendar in Heqing, Yunnan each year. This pilgrimage ceremony is related to the origin of Heqing.

As the story goes, Muni, the grand chancellor of Tibetan King had a son named Mou Gatuo, who was Buddha descended to the world, and the son was proficient in Buddhist sutras, and was favored by Tibetan King. At that time, Tibetan King wanted to ally with White King, and appointed Mou Gatuo as the envoy. Mou Gatuo asked a string of Buddha's relics and Muni beads from Panchen, brought presents including natural wine, Tibetan grapes, turtles, dogs, Tibetan horses and peal and headed towards Dali.

When passing by North Mountain in Jianchuan and West Mountain in Heqing, Mou Gatuo saw vast sea, and he said, "I must drain sea water and open up a new field."

When he arrived in Dali, White King saw Mou Gatuo who had outstanding talent and appearance, and wanted him to be his son-in-law. He made three requests to White King: firstly, White King shall make peace with Tibetan King permanently; secondly, a sutra tower will be built for him and he can still chant sutras and practice meditation after marriage; thirdly, he shall be free after marriage. White King accepted his requests. After the marriage, Mou Gatuo cultivated himself every day and didn't enter the inner court, and the princess wasn't satisfied and complained to her parents about the wrong marriage. White King asked Mou Gatuo about it, he said that he was devoted to cultivation, so that he could rebuild Yangtongluo and turn it into a good field. After hearing his words, White King wanted to test his strength. Mou Gatuo carried a large stone from an artificial hill to the scripture hall easily. White King was surprised, agreed at his intention, and ordered others to go to Zhonghe Peak of Diancang Mountain and bring back the tin stick and meditaion cushion which were left by Guanyin when creating Dali.

Mou Gatuo bid farewell to the princess, and she went to Shangguan to see him off. Mou Gatuo said to the princess, "Good bye!" The princess asked him to leave a memorial, he took out a withered

说：我一定要排干海水，开辟出一个新坝子来！

到了大理，白王见牟伽陀才貌出众，要招他为驸马。牟伽陀向白王提出三个要求：第一，要白王与藏王永世和平相处；第二，给他造一座经塔，婚后仍念经参禅；第三，婚后，让他自由自在。白王都一一答应了。结婚以后，牟伽陀天天修道，不进内宫，公主不满意，埋怨爹妈把事做错了。白王去问牟伽陀，牟伽陀说，他一心修道，好去开辟漾统罗，让它变成良田。白王听了，就想试试他已经修得了多大本领。牟伽陀毫不费力就把假山上一块大石头搬到了经堂。白王很惊讶，就赞成了牟伽陀的打算，并问他需要些什么?牟伽陀说："只要一根锡杖，一个蒲团。"白王就叫人到点苍山中和峰上，取来了观音开辟大理时留下的锡杖和蒲团。

牟伽陀向公主告别，公主送他到上关。牟伽陀对公主说："你转回去罢。"公主要他留下一件

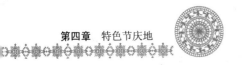

纪念的东西，牟伽陀顺手从行李中取出一朵烂纸花给她，公主不高兴，顺手把它插在一朵野花上，这花马上就活起来，长成了花上花，后来人们都叫这种花为"和尚花"。

牟伽陀来到鹤庆西南角的金斗山修炼。山脚下有个村子叫崖村，村里有个樵夫张小乙，天天上山打柴，看见牟伽陀一天到晚坐在那里不吃不动，以为是妖魔。一天，张小乙壮起胆子去问，牟伽陀就把他准备排干海水的心愿说了。当时，崖村正闹旱灾，准备开坛求雨。张小乙回到村里，叫村人请牟伽陀来求雨。牟伽陀用锡杖往地下一插，立刻现出一口菩提井，又解下一个牟尼珠放在地下，立刻长出了一棵菩提树。从此，人们都非常尊敬牟伽陀。金斗山下其他村子的人也要来接牟伽陀去，甚至为了这事发生口角。牟伽陀就说，来金斗山就是为了开辟海子，对大家有利，大家为这点事争执，就不

paper flower form his package and gave it to her, she was unpleased and inserted it into a wild flower, the paper flower was alive immediately and turned into a flower in flower, and people called it "monk's flower" afterwards.

Mou Gatuo came to Jindou Mountain at the southwest corner of Heqing to cultivate vital energy. There was a village called Ya Village at the foot of the mountain, a woodcutter named Zhang Xiaoyi lived in the village, and he saw Mou Gatuo sitting there motionlessly without eating anything and thought that he was a demon. One day, Zhang Xiaoyi ventured to ask him and Mou Gatuo told him about his wish to drain sea water. At that time, Ya Village was suffering from server drought, and prepared an altar to pray for rain. Zhang Xiaoyi retuned to the village and asked villagers to invite Mou Gatuo to pray for rain. Mou Gatuo inserted the tin stick into the ground, a Bodhi well appeared at once, he took out a Muni bead and put it under the ground and a Bodhi tree grew up immediately. Hereafter, People respected Mou Gatuo very much. People form other villlages under Jindou Mountain invited Mou Gatuo and even quarreled about it, Mou Gatuo said that he came to Jindou Mountain to drain the sea, which would be beneficial for all people and he would be unpleased if they quarreled about such trifles. He named the village in the south

Yingyi Village and named the village in the north Heyi Village and all people were pleased.

One day, Mou Gatuo went out, saw two strong men wrestling and helped them smooth it out. One was named Shi Ganliude and was a manson of Potouyi Village. The other named Jin Dayingshen was a peasant at the foot of West Mountain. Their fathers died when they were young and they took good care of their mothers.The manson pastured the cattle on the slope and fell asleep and the cattle ate the wheat of the Jin Family.Jin Dayingshen was so angry that he plucked up a large palm tree to beat the cattle. The manson woke up with a start, held the two legs of the cattle and carried it to run. Jin Dayingshen caught him up and they were locked in a duel. Persuaded by Mou Gatuo repeatedly, the two persons became reconciled. Mou Gatuo inquired about the sea, both of them said that there had been a tadpole dragon raising winds and waves and endangering common people. It would raise up its head on August 15th every year. This dragon must be conquered if he wanted to drain the sea. Mou Gatuo was very pleased, and he gave some money to them and asked them to attend to their mothers and help him when he was going to drain the sea. They were glad and were willing to take him as their master.

符我的本意了。他就给南面的村子取名迎邑村，给北边的村子取名和邑村，大家都高兴了。

一天，牟伽陀出来玩，看见两个大力士在搏斗，就去劝解。原来，一个名叫石干六得，是破头邑村的石匠。一个名叫金大硬神，是西山脚底的庄稼汉。两个人都早就死了父亲，都很孝顺寡母。这天，石匠在山坡上放牛，睡了一觉，牛吃了金家的麦子。金大硬神生气了，拔起一棵大棕树就来打石匠放的牛。石匠被惊醒，连忙跑来捉起牛的两腿往背上一背就跑。金大硬神赶上前来，两人就打得难分难解。经牟伽陀再三劝解，两人也就和好了。牟伽陀打听海里的情况，两人都说：多年来有条蝌蚪龙，不时兴风作浪，危害百姓。每年八月十五，它就要露出头来。如果要开辟这个海子，必须先降伏这条龙。牟伽陀听了很高兴，给了他们一些钱，叫他们好好侍奉母亲，又约他们两人，将来开辟海子时来帮忙。两人很高兴，情愿拜牟伽陀做师父。

不几天，牟伽陀去拜访石干六得，刚好石干六得牵着牛回家来。牛一见牟伽陀，不敢往前走，石匠就把牛抱起来丢进牛圈。进了家，没有凳子，石匠从门外搬进两个大石头，牟伽陀坐。坐了一会，牟伽陀又约石干六得去访金大硬神，谁知金大硬神上山砍柴去了，他母亲正眼巴巴盼着儿子回来呢。二人等了一会，才见他抱着一棵大树回来。牟伽陀就约起两个大汉来到海子边。两个大汉说，海子太大，咋个排得干啊！牟伽陀也有些动摇了。

观音怕牟伽陀灰心，化身成一个老婆婆，来到金斗山下。一天，牟伽陀又约了两个大汉来看海子，在小河边碰见个老婆婆在洗衣服。老婆婆说："我把衣服浮到河心，你能叫得转它，就可以凿山排海水了。不然，只是

Several days later, Mou Gatuo went to visit Shi Ganliude and Shi just led the cattle to go home. The cattle saw Mou Gatuo and didn't dare to go ahead and the manson carried the cattle and threw it into the cattle housing. Mou Gantuo entered the house, but there were no chairs, the manson carried two huge outdoor stones into the house and Mou Gantuo was seated. After a while, Mou Gatuo asked Shi Ganliude to visit Jin Dayingshen, but Jin Dayingshen went to the mountain to cut wood. His mother was waiting for him. After a while, they saw him coming back with a big tree. Mou Gatuo invited the two men to go to the sea. They said that the sea was too vast to drain. Mou Gatuo was dispirited somewhat.

Guanyin feared that Mou Gatuo was disheartened, and she turned into an old woman and came to the foot of Jindou Mountain. One day, Mou Gantuo invited the two men to see the sea and met an old woman near the stream. The old woman said, "You can cut through mountains and drain sea water if you can rotate back the clothes which I float on the river. Otherwise, it would just be a whim." Mou Gatuo did so, but the clothes couldn't rotate back. The clothes rotated back at once when the old woman called. Mou Gatuo felt sad.

Several days later, Mou Gatuo came to the stream, and saw the old woman grinding a big iron rod on a stone. He asked," Why do you grind such a big iron rod?" The old woman answered, "I grind it into an embroidery needle." He asked, "Is it possible?"She said, "If you work on it hard enough,you can grind an iron bar into a needle." Mou Gatuo thought it over, "I will not lose heart." He decided to move from Jindou Mountain to Shibao Mountain and cultivate himself for ten years, and then he could cut through South Mountain and drain sea water.

The parents of Mou Gatuo were worried because he didn't come back for a long time, and led people and horses to come to Dali to look for him. When they came to Jianchuan, they died of illness because they were not accustomed. It's said that their tombs can be seen in Jianchuan now.

Mou Gatuo came to Shibao Mountain, and the Ling Mountain God knew his wish of draining sea water. The Ling Mountain God was the god of East Mountain. and local people named him Lord Ling Mountain. He turned into a local man to visit Mou

空想。"牟伽陀照着做，衣服不会转来。老婆婆一叫，衣裳马上转来了。牟伽陀心里很不好过。

隔几天，牟伽陀又来到小河边，又碰上老婆婆在水边石头上磨大铁棒。牟伽陀问："这么粗的铁棒，磨它干什么？"老婆婆说："磨成绣花针。"牟伽陀说："咋个磨得成！"老婆婆说："只要功夫深，铁杵磨成针！"牟伽陀想了想：这是要自己不灰心啊!他就决定从金斗山迁到石宝山去，再苦炼十年，修好道法，再来开凿南山，排干海水！

却说，牟伽陀的父母见儿子久久不回，心里很焦急，就带领人马去大理寻找。走到剑川，水土不适，老两口就病死了。据说，现在剑川还有他们的坟墓哩。

牟伽陀到了石宝山，他要排干海水的事被灵山神知道了。灵山神是东山的山神，本地百姓叫他灵山老爷。他化装成一个本地人去访牟伽陀，石干六得和金大硬神把守山门，不许他进去。牟伽陀已经知道是山神来访，就叫两个弟子让他进来。灵山神还自称"土人"，牟伽陀立刻把他的来历点破，并希望他帮助排海开坝。灵山老爷冷笑说："这么个汪洋大海，咋个排法?你牟伽陀果真开出坝子，我的脸永远不朝西!"话说到这个地步，两人也就不欢而别了。后来，鹤庆坝子开辟出来了，灵山神真个是背朝坝子，不好意思看鹤庆了。

牟伽陀去石宝山时，老百姓舍不得他，他就告诉老百姓说："我不是离开你们，你们每年来石宝山看看我，也就行了。"

直到今天，当地人为了纪念这位把海子变成坝子，又教会人类种植稻谷的牟伽陀，每年农历的三月初三，当地人总要带上供品，去石宝山朝拜它，还烧香烧纸，祈求他继续保佑鹤庆风调雨顺，年年有大丰收。

Gatuo, Shi Ganliude and Jin Dayingshen guarded the gate and didn't allow him to come into it. Mou Gatuo had kown that the mountain god visited him, and asked his two disciples to let him in. The Ling Mountain God called himself "native people".Mou Gatuo laid bare his purpose of the visit at once, and hoped that he could help him drain the sea and open up a field. Lord Ling Mountain sneered, "How to drain such vast sea? I will never face to the east if you can open up a field."After saying such words, they parted in discord. Afterwards, Heqing Dam was opened up, and the Ling Mountain God turned back against the dam, and was ashamed of seeing Heqing.

Before Mou Gatuo went to Shibao Mountain, common people were reluctant to part with him, so he told them, "I will not leave you, and you can come to Shibao Mountain to see me every year."

Local people commemorate Mou Gatuo who turned the sea into the field and taught human beings to plant paddy rice, they bring offerings to go to Shibao Mountain and burn incenses and papers, ask him to continue to bless people in Heqing and pray for great harvest on lunar March 3rd every year.

The Postscript of *Chinese Festival Culture Series*

China has developed its splendid and profound culture during its long history of 5000 years. It has a vast territory, numerous ethnic groups as well as the colorful festivals. The rich festival activities have become the invaluable tourism resources. The traditional festivals, such as the Spring Festival, the Tomb-Sweeping Day, the Dragon Boat Festival, the Mid-Autumn Day and the Double-Ninth Festival as well as the festivals of ethnic minorities, are representing the excellent traditional culture of China and have become an important carrier bearing the spirits and emotions of the Chinese people, the spirit bond of the national reunification, national unity, cultural identity and social harmony, and an inexhaustible driving force for the development of the Chinese Nation.

In order to spread the excellent traditional culture of China and build the folk festival brand for our country, the Folk Festival Commission of the China Union of Anthropological and Ethnological Science (CUAES) has worked with the Anhui People's Publishing House to publish the *Chinese*

《中国节庆文化》丛书后记

上下五千年的悠久历史孕育了灿烂辉煌的中华文化。中国地域辽阔，民族众多，节庆活动丰富多彩，而如此众多的节庆活动就是一座座珍贵丰富的旅游资源宝藏。在中华民族漫长的历史中所形成的春节、清明、端午、中秋、重阳等众多传统节日和少数民族节日，是中华民族优秀传统文化的历史积淀，是中华民族精神和情感传承的重要载体，是维系祖国统一、民族团结、文化认同、社会和谐的精神纽带，是中华民族生生不息的不竭动力。

为了传播中华民族优秀传统文化，打造中国的优秀民族节庆品牌，中国人类学民族学研究会民族节庆专业委员会与安徽人民出版社合作，在国务院新闻办公室的大力支持下，决定联合出版大型系列丛书——《中国节庆文化》丛书。为此，民族节庆专委会专门成立了《中国节庆文化》丛书编纂委员会，邀请了国际节庆协会（IFEA）主席兼首席执行官史蒂文·施迈德先生、中国文联执行副主席冯骥才先生、中国人类学民族学研究会常务副会长周明甫先生、国家民委政研室副主任兼中国人类学民族学研究会秘书长黄忠彩先生、国家民委文宣司司长武翠英女士等担任顾问，由文化部民族民间文艺发展中心主任李松担任主编，十六位知名学者组成编委会，负责丛书的组织策划、选题确定、体例拟定和作者的甄选。随后，组委会在全国范围内，遴选了五十位节庆领域知名专家学者以及有着丰富实操经验的节庆策划师共同编著。

策划《中国节庆文化》丛书，旨在弘扬中国传统文化，挖掘本土文化和独特文化，展示中华民

Festival Culture Series under the support from the State Council Information Office. For this purpose, the Folk Festival Commission has established the editorial board of the *Chinese Festival Culture Series*, by inviting Mr. Steven Wood Schmader, the president and CEO of the International Festival and Events Association (IFEA); Mr. Feng Jicai, the executive vice-president of China Federation of Literary and Art Circles; Mr. Zhou Mingfu, the vice-chairman of the China Union of Anthropological and Ethnological Science (CUAES); Mr. Huang Zhongcai, the deputy director of the politics research office of the National Ethnic Affairs Commission, and the secretary-general of the China Union of Anthropological and Ethnological Science (CUAES); Ms. Wu Cuiying , the director of the Cultural Promotion Department of the National Ethnic Affairs Commission as consultants; Li Song, the director of the Folk Literature and Art Development Center of the Ministry of Culture as the chief editor; and 16 famous scholars as the members to organize, plan, select and determine the topics and determine the authors. After the establishment of the board, 50 famous experts and scholars in the field of festivals and the festival planners with extensive experiences have been invited to jointly edit the series.

The planning of the *Chinese Festival Culture Series* is to promote the traditional Chinese culture, explore the local and unique cultures, showcase the charms of the festivals of the Chinese Nation, express the gorgeous and colorful folk customs and create a festival image for cities. The target consumers of the series are the readers both at home and abroad who are interested in the festivals of China, and the purpose of the series is to promote the traditional culture and modern culture of China to the world and make the world know China in a better way by using the festivals as medium. The editorial board requests the editors shall integrate the theories into practice and balance the expertise and the popularity.

At present, the first part of the series will be published, namely the *Festivals in Spring*, and the editorial work of this part has been started in April, 2012 and completed in June, 2013. During this period of time, the editorial board has held six meetings to discuss with the authors and translators in terms of the compiling styles, outlines, first draft and translation to improve the draft and translation; and to consult with the publishing house in terms of the graphic design, editorial style and publishing schedule to improve the cultural quality of the series.

The first part *Festivals in Spring* is composed of 10 volumes to introduce 10 folk festivals of China from the first month to the third month of the Chinese Calendar, including the Spring Festival, the Lantern Festival, the Festival of February of the Second, the Festival of March the Third, the Tomb-Sweeping Day, the Peony Festival, the

族的节庆魅力，展现绚丽多姿的民俗风情，打造节庆城市形象。本丛书以对中国节庆文化感兴趣的中外读者为对象，以节庆活动为载体，向世界推广中国的传统文化和现代文化，让中国走向世界，让世界更了解中国。编委会要求每位参与编写者，力争做到理论性与实践性兼备，集专业性与通俗性于一体。

目前推出的是第一辑《春之节》，其编纂工作自2012年4月启动，2013年6月完成。期间编委会先后六次召开了专题会议，就丛书编纂体例、书目大纲、初稿、译稿与作者及译者进行研讨，共同修改完善书稿和译稿；就丛书的装帧设计、编辑风格、出版发行计划与出版社进行协商，集思广益，提高丛书的文化品位。

《春之节》共十册，分别介绍了中华大地上农历一月至三月有代表性的十个民族节庆，包括春节、元宵节、二月二、三月三、清明节、牡丹节、藏历年、壮族蚂蚁节、苗族姊妹节、彝族赛装节等，对每个节日的起源与发展、空间流布、节日习俗、海外传播、现代主要活动形式等分别进行了详细的介绍和深度的挖掘，呈现给读者的将是一幅绚丽多彩的中华节庆文化画卷。

这套丛书的出版，是民族节庆专业委员会和安徽人民出版社合作的结晶。安徽人民出版社是安徽省最早的出版社，有六十余年的建社历史，在对外传播方面走在全国出版社的前列；民族节庆专业委员会是我国节庆研究领域唯一的国家级社团，拥有丰富的专家资源和地方节庆资源。这套丛书的出版，实现了双方优势资源的整合。丛书的面世，若能对推动中国文化的对外传播，促进传统民族文化的传承与保护，展示中华民族的文化魅力，塑造节庆的品牌与形象有所裨益，我们将甚感欣慰。

掩卷沉思，《中国节庆文化》丛书凝聚着诸位作者的智慧和学养，倾注

Tibetan Calendar New Year, the Maguai Festival of the Zhuang People, the Sister Rice Festival, and the Saizhuang Festival of the Yi Ethnic Group. Each festival is introduced in detail to analyse its origin, development, distribution, customs, overseas dissemination and major activities, showing the readers a colorful picture about the Chinese festivals.

This series are the product of the cooperation between the Folk Festival Commission and the Anhui People's Publishing House. Anhui People's Publishing House is the first publishing house of its kind in Anhui Province, which has a history of more than 60 years, and has been in the leading position in terms of foreign publication. The Folk Festival Commission is the only organization at the national level in the field of the research of the Chinese festivals, which has rich expert resources and local festival resources. The series have integrated the advantageous resources of both parties. We will be delighted and gratified to see that the series could promote the foreign dissemination of the Chinese culture, promote the inheritance and preservation of the traditional and folk cultures, express the cultural charms of China and build the festival brand and image of China.

In deep meditation, the *Chinese Festival Culture Series* bears the wisdoms and knowledge of all of its authors and the great effort of the editors, and explains the splendid cultures of the Chinese Nation. We hereby sincerely express our gratitude to the members of the board, the authors, the translators, and the personnel in the publishing house for their great effort and to all friends from all walks of the society for their support. We hope you can provide your invaluable opinions for us to further promote the following work so as to show the world our excellent festival culture.

Editorial Board of
Chinese Festival Culture Series
December, 2013

着编纂者的心血和付出，也诠释着中华民族文化的灿烂与辉煌。在此，真诚感谢各位编委会成员、丛书作者、译者、出版社工作人员付出的辛勤劳动，以及各界朋友对丛书编纂工作的鼎力支持！希望各位读者对丛书多提宝贵意见，以便我们进一步完善后续作品，将更加璀璨的节庆文化呈现在世界面前。

《中国节庆文化》
丛书编委会
2013年12月